THE
LITTLE
Hierophant

2019 poetry collection

ERIC NIXON

Cover design and back photo of Charlie Barker by Eric Nixon.
Author photo by Kari Chapin.

© 2020 by Eric Nixon

ISBN-13: 978-0-9984362-4-1
BISAC: Poetry / American / General

All rights reserved. No part of this book may be copied, reproduced, stored in a retrieval system, or transmitted in any form or by any process without first obtaining written permission from the author; the exception being a reviewer who may quote brief passages with appropriate credit.

That being said, I'm pretty flexible with fully credited adaptations. Please contact me if you are considering adapting or remixing any works contained within this book.

All situations depicted in this book are products of the author's imagination and may not match any reality known to otherwise exist elsewhere.

Published by Double Yolk Press in South Deerfield, MA.
EricNixonAuthor@gmail.com

EricNixon.net

DEDICATION

This book is dedicated to Charlie Barker, the little hierophant.

POET'S FOREWARD

Hello!

2019 was a big poetry year for me. Probably my biggest so far.

Every year the Beals Preserve in Southborough, Massachusetts holds a summer-long event called Art On The Trails where local artists set up art installations throughout their trail system. After the art is up, they have a call for poets to come, view the art, and write poetry based on the pieces that moved them. I entered several and four of my poems were accepted and published in their poetry collection, *On The Trails: Unexpected Gestures*. At the closing event, they had the poets read their poems in front of the works of art. This was the first time I've ever read my poetry in a public setting. My four poems (which are all in this collection you're holding) were: "Rainbow Wall," "My Need Is Your Taking," "Bouncing Ball," and "Strata."

2019 was also notable because three of my poems (from my 2018 collection, *Equidistant*), "Peak Summer," "The Momentum Of Existence," and "Reinvention," were read on Garrison Keillor's program, *The Writer's Almanac*. This was an incredible honor and is now the fifth time my poems have been featured.

And, 2019 is noteworthy because I not only wrote my *tenth* poetry collection, but it was also my biggest collection to date (technically my 2013 collection, *The Entire Universe* had more poems, but *The Little Hierophant* is much longer, page-wise). I have now written over 1,400 poems across all of my books.

Without further delay, I give you, *The Little Hierophant*.

Please enjoy and thank you!

Eric

TABLE OF CONTENTS

January – 9 poems
The Ones Won
The Janitor Whispered
I Was Heard
Ski Resort Guy
The One Put There By Your Gut
Rotary Volvo
Which Thought Is Screaming The Loudest
Waiting For The Storm
The Little Hierophant

February – 1 poem
The Traffic Light

March – 14 poems
The Potential A Weekend Holds
Conference On My Pillow
Your Focus
Nostalgia Is An Anchor
The Last Time I Heard Her Name
Tainted By The Flush
Winking Red Light
A Coffee To Get The Coffee
Her Favorite Thing
On A Vacation
The Best Vacation Ever
A Line Of Robins
These Cusping Weeks
They Didn't Get Far

April – 14 poems
Hint Of Damp
The Brush Stroked

Bedbug Smoke
Heading To Shamrock
Her Name Becomes
Can't Stop The Greening
Beyond The Ordinary
Peepers
A Splash Of Vibrancy
Zero…And Then Everything
Butterflies And Bees
Silence
The Line
A Toothpaste Cat

<u>May</u> – 10 poems
Between Birthdays
Walls
Exquisitely Energetic
The Universe Broke My Game
I saw The Bunny
I Normally Just Potato
Locally Hated
Thunderhead Far In The Distance
But, It's In A Tube!
A Shadow Still Remains

<u>June</u> – 14 poems
Refreshing
The Exact Same Newspaper
Now Is The Later
You Have To Watch It
I Meant To Watch
Party Boy
Suffer The Speed
Little Wet Baby Bunny
What Are
Empty Kayak
Wishing Circles

You Are Not Here To Coast
Back A Page
Rainbow Wall

July – 30 poems
New Keyboard
Mine
Cloud In My Yard
Power Button
My Need Is Your Taking
The Moments Of Uncharacteristic Bravery
I Felt Like I Slept Through An Entire Generation
Bouncing Ball
Galaxies Are Stepping Stones
The Dude On The Motorcycle
Because Of My Beep
I Want To Be A Do-er
Pringle Fountain
The New Car Feel
I Bear Witness
Unknown To Forgotten
Cats Are Conditional
Watching The Wind
My Fitbit Is Lowering Its Expectations
The Last Lightning Bug
I Felt The Universe
Strata
(a parenthetical poem)
It's Completely Up To Me
Honkin'
Malaise Of Choice
Always Missing
What Am I Doing Here?
Every Day
Separation

<u>August</u> – 32 poems
Moments Like This
Expressing Creativity
Fully, Completely, Forever And Ever
That Iridescent
The Interplay Between
Hoover Damn
Time Is A Bullet
Low Row
Determination
Action Is Happening
It Comes As No Surprise
A Grandfather Clock
The Hot Air Balloon
The Delicate Nuance
One One-Thousandth Of A Percent
Trusted To Flush
Scale Models
I'm Glad She Sat Elsewhere
A Daddy Longlegs
I Want My Days To Mean Something
Dear Dave In Baltimore
Frogs Or Flags
Such Triviality
Disquieted
The Purpose
Feeling The Connection
Gut Reaction
Steady Hearty Breeze
Stalled
The Screen Saver Factory
A Well-Sculpted Topiary
The Dulling

<u>September</u> – 26 poems
Summer Is Over Today
$7.11
The Slow Let-Go

Fortune I had Taped Over
With American Eyes
Caught In Pause
Giggle Her
Luckily It's Only A Half Moon
The Red Leaf
The Sad Shame Of A Society
Parroting
Letting The Words Blur
The Energy Of The Moment
Melted With The Knowing
Mini-Mercury
Long Shadows
Brilliant Highlights
Dresses Are Made To Come Off
The Doorway Of Expression
Fluffy Cloud, Solid Chunk
Energy Is Elastic
Passivity
Every Poem Is A Brick
Foliage Delivery
Mouse Pad
Sweet Caressing Silence

<u>October</u> – 30 poems
Good Citizen
Shorting The Future Of Time
The Sin Is Rising
The Stark Loss Of Contrast
Feeling The Echoing Glimmer
I Feel Like I Could Be
My Tiny Corner
Personification
Hue Of Blue
My Job As A Poet
Peeking At The Peak
The Changeover
Mid-October Killed It All

The Color Came Down
More Coverage
Warmth, Beauty, Fries, And Frosties
My Duty
Wherever It Takes Me
The Past Forgotten
The Short Answer To The Question Never Asked
To See A Flower
Trusting The Clouds
Cursed
One In A Million
The Unequivocal Reassurance
Faded Beauty
The Unseen Forces
Watching The Cornfield
The Only Thing I Know
What If I Wrote

<u>November</u> – 24 poems
Old New England
The Proudly Quippy Smartass
The Darkness Thoroughly Enjoys
Finding My Way
Ensconced By Handrails
Blank Clean
Faster Than We Can Dream
Living With The Bruises
Now Is The Lull
Risking It
Your Words Will Be On Walls
The Reverby Twang
Disposable
Buy Into
Immutable
The Potential
Traffic Cameras
The Little Smudge
Snowflake

New Moon
Past Nouns
Connecting To The Source Of Myself
Speaking In Tongues
The Most American Of Holidays

December – 26 poems
The Little Quips
Making My Way Up Again
A Huge Snowman
Having Boundless Creativity
The Decorations Might Not Make It Up
Goodbye To The Teens
The Fire Under Your Ass
Library Mornings
The Environment You Choose
I Writhe My Time
Between The Sure-Footing Spots
Ejector Seat
The Smallest Flake
Caught In The Spray
Flip The Page Over Into January
A Brittle Twig
I Like How The Neighbor Keeps His Outdoor Trees Lit At Night
A Regular Day
Band Names From The 1980s
My Penmanship
Look Better On Paper
I Was Born Way Back
Puddle Now
All Of This Speaks Of Spring
This Was Meant To Be Seen
At The End

2019 total: 230

JANUARY

The Ones Won

2018 had built itself up
Day by day, on top of days,
Stacking into weeks,
And rising into months
Until it reached its upper limit,
The point where it could grow no longer
And, just like that,
Humanity hit the reset button
And the hundreds of numbers
Were gone in an instant
And the ones won

                January 1, 2019
                Whately, Massachusetts

All ones, all the time – today only.

Update: November 11th just emailed me and said that's not true and I should do a little research before I make unfounded proclamations like that (I don't know how November 11th got my email address – that kind of weirds me out a little).

January

The Janitor Whispered

As I walked past the bowl
That someone in the office
Randomly fills with candy
I reached for a peanut butter cup
And I honestly could have sworn
I heard the man I just passed
In the hall a few feet behind me
Say something indistinct, if at all,
The man, the janitor, whispered,
"Don't do it," barely audible,
So faintly it was like telepathy
But despite his magical means
I was not dissuaded in the least

            January 8, 2019
            Whately, Massachusetts

I really like peanut butter cups.

I Was Heard

As my meditation simmered down
And the energy coursed through me
Like some kind of movie superhero
I uplifted the most sincere thought
A "thank you" to the Universe
And I felt, at once, I was heard

        January 8, 2019
        Whately, Massachusetts

Been having a lot of stunning meditation sessions lately. I don't know what's up with that, but I'm happy.

January

Ski Resort Guy

Ski resort guy
Turtleneck on and up
Like his feathered blond hair
As he leaned back in his chair
At a half-sideways angle
His legs casually crossed
Right hand resting on his thigh
The other arm, outstretched,
Tapping mindlessly on the table
Drawing attention to his presence
Looking like he was lounging
The evening away in the posh bar
Of an unnecessarily upscale ski resort
And then was instantly teleported here,
For some completely unknown reason,
To this Whole Foods café eating area
A good hundred miles from
Where I assume he belongs

>January 8, 2019
>Hadley, Massachusetts

I would not have been surprised if he had a pair of ski boots sitting in a melted puddle beside him.

As a side-note, I apparently can't spell "resort" correctly. Every time I typed it I wrote "resport."

The One Put There By Your Gut

The dawning perception
That life is precious
That it is not meant
To be squandered or wasted
A concept that seems
So stupidly simple but
Is so incredibly difficult
To actually actualize
When you're stuck
Entirely too deep
In the thing you're in
Which seemed
Like such a good thing
At the time
Back when you were
Ticking off checkmarks
Under the *PROS* column
Like nobody's business
And now, it's still true,
But there is just that one
Sitting there under *CONS*
Chewing at your consciousness
The one put there by your gut
Who, in the end, instinctually,
Is the all-knowing decider,
And is always right

     January 19, 2019
     Whately, Massachusetts

January

Rotary Volvo

Every day
Whether or not
I'm a little early,
Right on time,
Or a little late,
The same red Volvo
Enters the same rotary
From the road to my right
Going the opposite way
Of me in my silver Volvo
So now it's become a thing
Where, every day,
I am always looking
With great expectation
For my rotary Volvo
Mirroring my morning routine

          January 19, 2019
          Whately, Massachusetts

It's weird, but neat.

Which Thought Is Screaming The Loudest

I don't write
To satiate
Other people's expectations
I only write
For myself
As a way of
Expressing my experiences
Through the chaotic process
Determined by
Which thought
Is screaming the loudest
To be let out

        January 19, 2019
        Whately, Massachusetts

January

Waiting For The Storm

I'm waiting for the storm
That's supposed to drop
A foot or two of snow,
Ice, sleet, rain, and cats.
Standing at the sink
I look out the window over
The expansive field
Quiet in its off-season
Dull olive-tinged emptiness
And I feel compelled
To take "Before"
And "After" photographs
To post on my Instagram

>January 19, 2019
>Whately, Massachusetts

I think having a camera in your pocket 24/7, combined with instant access to social media is really changing the way we think and how we react to life.

I did not take before and after photos.*

*But I might. There's still time.

The Little Hierophant

Trying to sum up the life
Of the little hierophant
Who ruled the hearts of us
Is an utterly impossible task
With his happy-go-lucky walk
His need for belly scratches
The tenderness he showed
To his two favorite toys
Bunny the bunny and
Andy the hedgehog –
Carrying them around
Wherever he went,
Making sure they
Got plenty of time
By the food and water,
Arranging them carefully
In the morning sunbeams,
Putting them in front of
The heater in the winter;
The way he fearlessly
Power-pawed the door
To bust in after every walk,
The way he stood up strong
(Despite being so little short)
To every perceived threat
While on our nightly strolls,
The enthusiasm he showed
With every waking moment,
How his tail never stopped –
A blur in every single picture.
This was a creature who taught
Two heedless humans
How to live life joyfully
And to appreciate every second –
From when we first held
The young boy in Vermont
To that very last moment

January

Tonight at the vet's office
When the tail finally stopped
And he went zooming off
On his next big adventure.
Honestly, I can't encapsulate
For you in a neat and tidy way
A life lived as an exclamation point,
Only that the little soul of that dog
Filled us with the kind of happiness
We've never known before
And taught us to live, love, and enjoy
This amazing life we've been given

    January 24, 2019
    Whately, Massachusetts

Charlie Parker Chapin Nixon
(also known as Charlie Barker)
May 2, 2005 to January 24, 2019

We love you and we miss you.

FEBRUARY

The Traffic Light

Waiting at the traffic light
That seems to be against me
As I watched the other traffic
Get the green for far too long
So many cars flowing on by
Always getting the signal to go
While my light is stuck on no
So I sit and fiddle with the radio
And stew with jealousy aimed at the cars
Constantly coming and going
With incredibly unfettered ease
Frustrating because I want my turn
And it feels like I've been right here
Trapped in this same spot for years
Making me realize one of two things:
Either it is just completely broken
Or the light just doesn't like me

>February 28, 2019
>Northampton, Massachusetts

The other day I sat at a traffic light for an unusually long time. It was clearly not on a timer, which made me wonder if it was one of those weight-activated ones and I wasn't in the right spot for it to register me. Then I thought, *what if I was actually on the sensor but I didn't weigh enough?* That flattered me just enough to blush and smile, but after another two minutes, I got annoyed again, backed up, and repositioned the car. Thirty seconds later, the light changed. That's the trouble when the ground is covered with so much road salt you can't tell where the lines are.

February

The Little Hierophant

MARCH

The Potential A Weekend Holds

The potential a weekend holds
On a Friday afternoon
Is a thing of revered beauty;
Immense and unending
With so many possibilities
Each and every one of them
Completely do-able
And perfectly achievable…
Until you accidentally blink
Discovering two days passed
And the sad realization sets in
Of a weekend spent and gone
Sinks heavy in the heart
With the only indicator
Of its briefest existence
Is the dissipating aroma of
Its fumes, long since evaporated
Leaving a sticky residue of regret
Needing five days to scrub clean
Before the excitement can return

    March 1, 2019
    Northampton, Massachusetts

March

Conference On My Pillow

The new 3am ritual
As the cat hops up
And settles down
Wrapping around
My head, meowing
And loudly purring
That it's now time
For the conference
On my pillow
To begin

        March 1, 2019
        Northampton, Massachusetts

Bunny the cat is quite persistent.

Your Focus

Put your focus
On what you
Want so you
Get what you
Want which is
Better than
Focusing on
What you
Don't want
And getting
Exactly That

                March 1, 2019
                Northampton, Massachusetts

Nostalgia Is An Anchor

Nostalgia is an anchor
A weighty device
Meant to keep you
Completely immobile,
In one spot, in place,
Hopefully still above
The water's unforgiving
Horizontal line
Separating worlds
Which, if you dip under,
You will be easily
Down and drowned
Following the weight
To its resting spot
Where it is unlikely
You'll choose to move.
Whether or not
It is bound and
Tightly tethered
To your person
As it's dropped
Is completely up to you

        March 2, 2019
        Whately, Massachusetts

I woke up in the middle of the night with the phrase "Nostalgia is an anchor" at the forefront of my mind. I wrote it down and forgot about it until now when I looked at my phone's notes.

The Little Hierophant

The Last Time I Heard Her Name

The last time I heard her name
She was the little kid who lived
In the newly-built house
Directly across the street
From where I grew up
Where it used to be just forest
Then, the house, and the family
And this girl who I only know
From the few minutes each morning
Waiting for the school bus
At the end of my driveway
She seemed nice and very smart
And that's all I knew about her
Because we moved across town
And I never gave her another thought
Until this morning
When I saw the news
And recognized her name
Found dead in a house fire
Along with her three children
And her husband,
A name I also remembered,
A name police are saying
Murdered his family
And burned it all down
Before finishing himself as well
In a shocking ending
That no one saw coming

      March 15, 2019
      Northampton, Massachusetts

Justine Wilbur, from what it looked like you had a pretty amazing life. I'm so sorry that it ended in this terrible way.

Tainted By The Flush

Filling up the water bottle
From the bathroom sink
Because, for some reason,
It's a lot colder here
Than from the sink
In the break room
But while I'm filling it
I'm stricken with fear
As the water's flowing
When the slight dip
In water pressure
Is indicating someone
Somewhere else
Is flushing a toilet
And even though
I absolutely know
There's no way
The pipes are connected
In that way, I still
Worry that the water
Is somehow, someway
Tainted by the flush

    March 15, 2019
    Northampton, Massachusetts

It's so unreasonable, but so understandable and relatable.

Winking Red Light

Today I took a route
I normally don't take
Ending up at a light
That contained a strange
Winking red light
That wasn't quite a strobe
As it was more *on* than *off*
And it wasn't intentional
Since its pulsations
Changed in frequency,
Rate, and intensity
It just seemed happy
Doing its own thing
Dancing and putting
On a show for me
Until it got a chance
To take a break
When the green light
Took center stage
Who, by the way,
Took its job
Way more seriously
And stayed steady
Until I passed under
And out of view

        March 15, 2019
        Northampton, Massachusetts

True story.

March

A Coffee To Get The Coffee

These days you don't
Go out in the morning
Just to simply get a coffee
While on your way somewhere.
Those who are coffee-dependent
Need a coffee to get the coffee
So they make one at home
To sip while getting ready
Often known as the "starter cup"
Then they go out in public
To get the main-course coffee
From the corner donut shop
The one they've had their eye on
From the moment they woke up
And now, the day may begin

        March 16, 2019
        Whately, Massachusetts

I don't drink coffee, but I think the philosophy described above is somewhat bonkers.

Her Favorite Thing

Her favorite thing
Is hitting the reset switch
On everyone she meets
Over and over and over
Because she enjoys
The full-circle process:
Being the one responsible,
Initiating, taking charge,
Purposely, deliberately,
Making messes of things,
Being wild and careless
With things bigger
And more important
Than even life itself
Plowing through
The tipping point
Directing, causing
The desired results
To the same mutually
Profitable conclusion
Proudly appreciating,
Surveying the results
Of her deft handiwork
And cleaning it all up
Whereby every aspect
Has been fully restored,
Soul, self, appearance
Everything so neat, tidy
And blissfully happy
So she can move on
To the next project
And begin anew

March 16, 2019
Whately, Massachusetts

March

Just experimenting with something a little different.

On A Vacation

Been so long since I've been away
On a vacation of any kind to wherever
But in this place I'm at now
I don't have the time or the ability
So, physically, I can't go anywhere
But mentally, I am completely free
So off I go
And I started off slow
Afraid to cut loose
Until my mind crossed the line
And, in a new state, in a new place,
I'm a new person,
Waking up from the deep hibernation
Yawning off the layers of dust
And finally feeling the excitement
Building, rising, driving me forward
Going, visiting, seeing, exploring
Like I always used to love to do
So I picked up the pace
And increased the tempo
A million percent
Because when you feel this free
Anything and everything is possible
So that's what you do
Everything at once
Eventually realizing
I'm still the person,
The version of me,
I always used to be
Who used to travel
To exotic locations
Doing fascinating things
Because it turns out
I still have the desire
I still have the ability
And now I know
How to get out

March

And go on a vacation
Anytime I ever need to go
To change the scenery
For a crazy week or even for
A particularly boring work shift
It's always there
All I need to do it think
And I'm there

        March 25, 2019
        Northampton, Massachusetts

Traveling is so easy. You just go.

The Best Vacation Ever

The best vacation ever
Would be the one where
We would go everywhere
And do everything
Truly experiencing
And enjoying all there is
Like an endless buffet
Where you never get full
Sampling the entirety
The world has to offer
Without ever leaving
The comfort of home

    March 26, 2019
    Northampton, Massachusetts

I've had vacations on the brain lately (obviously – two poems in a row). It's been so many years since I've been on one.

I like writing two poems about the same thing back to back like this. It's interesting to see how I can write something that's so different about the same topic.

March

A Line Of Robins

A line of robins
One, two, three
All in a line
The first hopped
One, two, three
Quick little jumps
The second followed
One, two, three
Doing the same
The third waited
One, two, three
And then flew away

    March, 27, 2019
    Whately, Massachusetts

I saw this in the yard this evening.

These Cusping Weeks

The playful ebb and flow of the seasons
Back and forth between winter and spring
With the cold, below-freezing nights
And the warming, wakening days
Each having their temperaturing say
Equally impacting these cusping weeks
Until the widening one eventually wins

        March 28, 2019
        Northampton, Massachusetts

March

They Didn't Get Far

It was only a month or two ago
When I saw the last of the flocks
The migratory geese heading south
And now, life has clearly reversed
As the living Vs are flying north
Which makes me wonder where
They ended up going this year
Because they didn't get far
And couldn't have made it
To their normal wintering spot
Did they stop and do a U-turn
Somewhere in the Carolinas?
Did they see a thermometer
And decide it was too hot
Either way, they're back
Honking their way to Canada

           March 28, 2019
           Whately, Massachusetts

APRIL

Hint Of Damp

The ground is wet
But no rain's falling
From the gray ceiling
Nothing but a hint of damp
Swirling, moistening the air
Making breathing better
With a cool, bready thickness
That generously carries
An earthly freshness
Never ever found indoors

        April 7, 2019
        Whately, Massachusetts

Technically, this isn't a new poem but one I heavily edited from its previous incarnation. I wrote the original in October of 2015 when I lived in Portland, Oregon and it was included in my *Cascadia's Fault* poetry collection.

I saw that the Emily Dickinson Museum in nearby Amherst, Massachusetts is putting on a public art project called, "The Art Of Rain Poetry." They are selecting five poems, which will be stenciled on the pavement in public spaces in downtown Amherst with a special paint that is invisible, until it gets wet and reveals the poems. Pretty neat stuff.

I searched through my poems and found "Hint Of Damp," chopped about 50% of it out to get it to the 40-word limit, and submitted it for the project.

Let's see what happens...

They didn't choose it.

April

The Brush Stroked

The brush stroked
Across the canvas
The energy applied
In waves of color
Conveying the feeling
Displaying the intensity
To those touched
By the electricity
Of the experience
A glancing witness
So brief in time
But lasting forever
Buzzing so deeply
In the heart of the touched

   April 7, 2019
   Whately, Massachusetts

Recently, I started watching "The Travel Man" on Hulu. Great show. In one episode they go to a museum in Amsterdam and spend on an art tour, drawing, trying to copy masterpiece paintings on their small pads of paper. That got me thinking about how the artist wields such power with their brushstrokes. They apply swaths of paint and years later when people see the painting in person, they're affected after spending a few seconds looking at it. It makes me think of seeing the gigantic painting, "The Coronation Of Napoleon" at the Louvre. It's such a beautiful painting that has really struck and stayed with me after so many years.

Bedbug Smoke

Driving along a road
In our semi-rural town
I see moderate gray smoke
Up ahead, drifting from a yard
And across the road
Which got me excited
Thinking someone was burning leaves
A springtime smell I love so much –
Like woody, peaty, earthy smoky;
So I rolled down all the windows
And breathed in deeply as I passed –
Looking over and seeing the source
Was, in fact, not a pile of leaves
But a mattress, fully engulfed,
And on fire in the side yard
Sending what I can only assume
Was bedbug smoke into my lungs
Because why else would someone
Get the urge to burn a mattress
Right there in their yard?

    April 7, 2019
    Whately, Massachusetts

This actually happened when we were driving past a house in South Deerfield. Gee whiz!

April

Heading To Shamrock

The ground
Was white for months
Then patchy
Receding to full khaki
With spots of light brown
Now upgrading
To drab olive
While changing
To a pear-ish color
Before becoming
Full-on green
And heading to shamrock

        April 9, 2019
        Whately, Massachusetts

I've been trying to be acutely aware of the transition from winter to spring in every little detail.

Her Name Becomes

When I think
Of the word
Emily
An acronym
Immediately
Comes to mind
Whereupon
Her name becomes:

Evacuate
My
Incessantly
Leaking
Yacht

Which is an equally silly
And a prudent warning
If you happen to be
In that situation

        April 14, 2019
        Whately, Massachusetts

I was reminded of an acronym contest in my college's newspaper way back in the 90s. You had to some up with the best acronym for the word "EMILY." I came in second. A friend came in first with "Even Murderous Inmates Like Yo-yos", but also got a "pat on the back" for, "Elongated Members Induce Loud Yodels."

April

Can't Stop The Greening

Can't stop the greening
From spreading
And overtaking
Everything in the view
Because it's springing
Back from the freezing
And confidently marching
Through April
Like it owns the place

        April 14, 2019
        Whately, Massachusetts

Spring!

Beyond The Ordinary

I had a dream the other night
Where it felt like I was
Walking down a busy street
In some city I couldn't identify
On a rainy day with my head
Deep in a cloud of books
Fluttering, swirling around
Like a close, nebulous mist
And I was, strangely, somehow
Reading them all at once
But no one else could see,
Beyond the ordinary,
The real me absorbing
Learning, devouring dozens
Of books with my subconscious
While my normal self
Was walking around,
Going about my average life
While simultaneously
Doing this extraordinary thing
That was totally normal for me

        April 27, 2019
        Whately, Massachusetts

April

Peepers

Peepers
Being peepy
By the peepery
High-pitching
Their chorusy
Springy squeaky
For only a few weeks
So I listen for a while
Appreciating their song

        April 27, 2019
        Whately, Massachusetts

A Splash Of Vibrancy

A splash of vibrancy
As the first rays
Of the morning sun
Changed the scenery
Of those far-away trees
From muted and dull
Shades of drabnicity
To bright and orangey
Brilliant and fully-lit
Perfectly hashtagable
And Instagram-worthy

        April 27, 2019
        Whately, Massachusetts

April

Zero…And Then Everything

Much like the entire Universe
Bursting forth from the event
That was the Big Bang
For as long as you ever knew
The normal was nothing, nothing,
Zero…and then EVERYTHING
Bursting, exploding, forth
Occupying the emptiness
Filling the void with everything
That was once never known

    April 27, 2019
    Whately, Massachusetts

Butterflies And Bees

Spring is the time when
Butterflies and bees
Make their appearance
Fluttering and buzzing
Bumbling and flitting
Everywhere all the time
Making their presence
Known, seen, and felt
Everywhere all the time
So hastily laying
The groundwork
So busily preparing
The world for the time
Beyond this season
And past the summer

    April 30, 2019
    Whately, Massachusetts

They're everywhere!

April

Silence

Sometimes
What is most needed
Is silence
So the ears
And the mind
Can rest, relax, and recharge
Because after a while
The words
And the energy of them
Build, lodge, and stick
In the brain
Clogging like a pipe
That won't drain
Until peace and quiet
Finally comes
Like a liquid cleaner
Designed to clear out
This type of obstruction
And when it does,
In one flowing push,
The freedom felt
Is amazing

        April 30, 2019
        Whately, Massachusetts

The Line

The line
Separating
The halves
Is where
Care is
Needed
Otherwise
Unheeded
You could
Easily fall
Into the trap
Purposely
Set out
To capture
And ensnare
The victim,
Unsuspecting
Or otherwise,
Tripping,
Falling, or
Going down
Much too hard
And never
Ever be seen
Or heard from
Again

        April 30, 2019
        Whately, Massachusetts

Be vigilant!

April

A Toothpaste Cat

A decision made –
So big, so powerful
It ends up becoming
A notion unable
To be undone
Once the thought
Has been expressed
It's out there
In the world
Like a toothpaste cat
Free from the tube
And running around
Living a life
Never previously
Considered
Or imagined
To this moment
We're in right now

    April 30, 2019
    Whately, Massachusetts

The Little Hierophant

MAY

Between Birthdays

My brother's birthday is April 2
Four weeks (and three years) later
Is my birthday on April 30
When we're celebrating his
You can absolutely count on
Not being able to count on the weather
Because you can get one of five
Distinct seasons happening
Individually, or all at once,
But it will be some combination
Of snow, rain, or raw bitterness

As the weeks pass between birthdays
The seasons change and even out
And every year I can always rely
On the weather being beautiful
As spring is in mid-bounce
And filled with spectacular glory
With flowers blooming
Trees starting their bursting
With leaves half-out
Birds everywhere singing
The sun warmly shining
The temperature still cool
But in that comfortable place
That you long for in the winter
And wish for in the summer
In the midst of all of this
I smile with appreciative joy
Because I know this is *my* time
The little present this planet
Gives to me every year

    May 1, 2019
    Whately, Massachusetts

May

I love, love, love the place on the calendar where my birthday sits. From the date, to where the season sits, to the re-birthing of everything. I love it so much.

Walls

People who are hurt by others
Are scared of being hurt again
So, naturally, they want
To prevent it from repeating
So they build walls
To keep the bad ones out
To keep the pain out
To keep anything out
That could possibly
Inflict anything negative
Upon them again
And the walls will do that
Yes, they will accomplish
Their intended purpose
But what the builders
Are unable to see
Due to their grief
Or their clouded belief
Is what the wall is blocking
Is what the wall is preventing
From reaching them
Like the views
Of the beauty beyond
Now obscured
Like the contrast
Now blocked
Like the experiences
Now prevented
By the limiting restriction
Intended to protect
But instead restricts
The fullness of life
From ever getting in
So to those working
So hard building
Walls to keep things out
I appeal to you to please

May

Pick up a sledgehammer
Swing it as hard as you can
Smash the whole thing down
As if the soul of your life
Depended upon it
Because, in its truest sense
It does

        May 19, 2019
        Whately, Massachusetts

One of the things that made America so great to begin with is the fact that we let in all of the people from around the world. Immigrants built this country. To restrict people from entering out of fear is shortsighted and not taking the *big picture* into account.

Exquisitely Energetic

This morning my meditation
Was stunningly exquisitely energetic
From the moment I closed my eyes
And focused my mind and my breath
I was *filled* with such intense energy
Lifting me, making me feel buoyant
Raising me up above the density
Above the heaviness of this world
And I felt the worries, the fears,
The surprisingly deep pains
Melt away like ice on a hot day
And instead, they were replaced
With a knowing confidence,
An all-encompassing calmness,
And a deeply-rooted peacefulness
That radiated outward from me
Like bright-light electric power
Off a superhero from a movie
And has still stayed with me
Feeling perfectly content, happy,
And blissfully confident
Knowing that everything,
Everything, *everything*
Will all turn out
Better than expected

    May 19, 2019
    Whately, Massachusetts

A+ meditations like today's are very rare, but when they happen, WOW, it's so amazing.

May

The Universe Broke My Game

A few weeks ago, the online computer game
That I've played an average of an hour a day
For the past seven and a half years
Stopped working
One day it loaded just fine
And the next, it crashed while loading.
I've tried rebooting the game
I've tried rebooting the computer
I've tried uninstalling the game
And then re-installing it
I've tried uninstalling the game platform
And re-installing it
To no success at all
I've tried contacting technical support
From the gaming company
But they could not find any issues
With my system, with the game, or anything
And told me good luck in figuring it out
I've tried installed the game
On my wife's computer
Where it actually worked
But ran so poorly it was unplayable
I've tried so much except for giving in
And just accepting this oddly coincidental fate
Because the number of signs
The Universe has given me
To get my ass in gear
And write my next novel
Has been truly astounding
Everywhere I look
I see my book title
Either the full title: *2493*
Or variations of it
That my dyslexic mind
Sees and identifies instantly
So the only logical assumption
That I can come up with is that

The Universe broke my game
As a means to get me to get going
And get writing this book
So I'm going to do exactly that:
Take this as a sign,
Give in, and get writing

        May 19, 2019
        Whately, Massachusetts

True story.

I've played Team Fortress 2 for about an hour a night for the better part of eight years and all of a sudden, in the midst of *so many* coincidences and hints from the Universe to finish writing my next novel, the game stopped working on my computer. Just mine.

May

I Saw The Bunny

Looking past my dog
Right there, only
Twenty feet away
I saw the bunny
Thankfully,
He did not
And we returned
Inside without issue

        May 25, 2019
        Whately, Massachusetts

We have a lot of rabbits living around us. They actually seem interested in Baxter, but he rarely notices them, which I'm thankful for since miniature Dachshunds were bred for rabbit hunting.

I Normally Just Potato

I normally just potato
Spending my days
Doing nothing but
Basking in the inertia
Appreciating inactivity
Inspecting it carefully
Knowing it intimately
Wrapping myself in foil
And baking in the oven
Sunning myself nicely
In the warmth of lethargy
Before slathering myself
With the butter and bacon bits
Of sluggishness and apathy
Before I deeply procrastinate
By doing a whole lot of nothing

        May 25, 2019
        Whately, Massachusetts

So…I had originally written a poem called, "Missing The Inertia," based entirely on my misconception that the word "inertia" was akin to "momentum," but it turns out that it is actually an antonym, not a synonym. So, in an effort to pound the meaning of the word into my head, I wrote this.

Learning!

Locally Hated

The oversized black truck
Peeled out of its driveway
Without even a glance
In either direction to check
For traffic or to see if it was safe
Instead expecting others
To watch out and brake for him
Which I did, so hard it caused
Everything to slide off my seats
I looked up to see it speeding off
At an entirely unsafe velocity
With its extra-wide second set
Of unnecessary back tires
Over the double yellow line
And the custom sticker
In the oddly-scripty font
Covering the entirety
Of the too-tinted back window
Rang true with a misplaced pride,
Arrogantly, contrarily bragging:
LOCALLY HATED

        May 25, 2019
        Whately, Massachusetts

Braggy assholes are still assholes.

Thunderhead Far In The Distance

Thunderhead far in the distance
Situated behind the large tree
In the back section of the yard
With the billowy puffed up parts
In the exact right proportions
In the exact right places
Giving it the distinct appearance
That the tree was, for some reason,
Wearing cute white fluffy bear ears
And now, I'll never see it
In the same way again

                May 27, 2019
                Whately, Massachusetts

But, It's In A Tube!

The other day I was
In the bathroom
Looking for ointment
To put on a cut
When I spied the tube
And discovered
It was not the ointment
But rather
A travel-sized toothpaste
And even though
I wasn't going to use it
My mind protested:
"But, it's in a tube!
 All stuff in tubes are the same!"
Which is not the case at all
But I still lingered over this
And considered the merits
Of my mind's logic
For a few seconds too long

        May 27, 2019
        Whately, Massachusetts

Secret thoughts.

A Shadow Still Remains

Pain leaves an impression
Deep
So deep
In its place
That when relief
Ultimately comes
And the pain has finally lifted
And is gone
A shadow still remains
Like a footprint
An indention in your spirit
Always there to remind you
How deep it once went
And the depths it'll go to
Next time

        May 27, 2019
        Whately, Massachusetts

May

The Little Hierophant

JUNE

Refreshing

This time
Of the year
Is so very
Refreshing
When the world
Wakes from winter
Finds, and discovers
Life blooming all around
Flooding the senses
With such feelings
Which haven't been felt
In too many seasons
And the merest act
Of breathing deeply
Inhaling the beauty
Each breath
Refreshing
Again and again
Refreshing
Filling the body
Replenishing
The vitality within
Refreshing
Reinvigorating
The heart
With something
Refreshing
Surrounding
With such Joy
Such buoyancy
So refreshing
That I
Just
Can't
Stop

June 1, 2019

June

Whately, Massachusetts

Spring!

The Exact Same Newspaper

At the busy hipstery coffee shop
Early on a Saturday morning
But just late enough to be busy
Sat an older couple over there
He, leaning back against the wall
An actual newspaper folded open
Like a giant butterfly spread out
Gray, with black splotchy bands
While across the table sat his wife
Reading the exact same newspaper
But discretely, compactly, on her iPad
Silently swiping to go to the next page
While everyone knew when he turned
Due to the awful ruckus and disruption
That the physical product brings about

          June 2, 2019
          Williamsburg, Massachusetts

An interesting scene at Bread Euphoria this morning.

June

Now Is The Later

There is no use
Holding back
Any longer
Because
Now is the later
I was saving for

        June 8, 2019
        Whately, Massachusetts

You Have To Watch It

When I tell people
"You *have* to watch it,"
About a TV show
I just discovered
And binged all weekend
They *need* to watch it
Because it's the best thing ever

When people tell me
"You *have* to watch it,"
About a TV show
They just discovered
And binged all weekend
They *need* to shut up about it
Because it's not anything
I'd ever be interested in

    June 9, 2019
    Whately, Massachusetts

It's funny how this works out. When me (or you, or anyone) discovers something awesome, you can't wait to tell *everyone* about it – but when others try to tell me about something awesome they saw on TV, I'm always thinking, *Uh, no thanks. Not interested. Please be quiet.*

Does that make me a little bit awful? Yes, but it's okay because you do it too.

June

I Meant To Watch

I meant to watch the seasons change
Much more closely
So I could report on their actions
And their progress
As one type of flower
Announced its presence
Fully bloomed
And finally passed
As another type
Went through its cycle
Like a slow-motion
Fireworks show
Taking place over weeks
And months
But they slipped by
So quickly
So easily
And every few days
I caught myself thinking
"I'll get a picture later"
Or
"I'll take notes tomorrow"
And then never did
So, before I knew it,
An entire season had passed
And so did my chance
To fully document
The blending of the season
As told by the flowers
Surrounding my home

    June 9, 2019
    Whately, Massachusetts

Note: despite the similar titles, this poem has nothing to do with the last one.

Party Boy

Sometimes I think I could be a musician
The kind that makes the insipid music –
Highly-energetic, with big bass,
And more electronic drums
Than you could dare to count
With the lyrics that they'll shout
In the party clubs on the shores
Where the overly manscaped
Fist-pumping bro-dudes
Drunkenly shout every word
"Yeah maaaaan,
 Who's the party boy?
 I'm the party boy!"
Over and over and over
For the full four minutes
Of the song I released
Under a pseudonym
Because I'm embarrassed
That anyone would find me out
As the guy who wrote
That piece of musical trash

Correction…
That *lucrative* piece of trash
Which funds my whole world

    June 9, 2019
    Whately, Massachusetts

Just speculation. I have not actually released any dance club hit songs.

Not yet…

Suffer The Speed

It's like God's cat
Sat on the remote of life
Unaware and unconcerned
With its paw squarely on
The *fast-forward* button
And we are the ones
Who suffer the speed
Whipping through
Months, years, decades
Like they were minutes
Watching kids grow
Up into adults too soon
Watching relatives
Shrink, age, and wither
And vanish too soon
And we're left wondering
What'll happen when
We're sped through
The end that comes
For every one of us

        June 9, 2019
        Whately, Massachusetts

Yesterday I went to the high school graduation party of the daughter of close friends. I've complained for years in my poetry collections about how unfair it is that time goes by *so quickly* and here was another painful example. I remember when she was born, and now, here I am at her high school graduation. I know the next time I blink, she'll be done with college. Too fast. Entirely too fast. It's just another reminder to fill every day with the things that matter. I think that's the only way to make it feel like days aren't blinking by like seconds.

Little Wet Baby Bunny

Little wet baby bunny
Sitting in the field
As the rain falls down
Doing nothing funny
But instead spending
Its time being cute
Which is actually
A reasonably good way
To while away the day

                June 16, 2019
                Whately, Massachusetts

What Are

What are
The eyes
Doing
Looking
At me
Because
They totally are
But
Never for long
As they scan
The forest
To see if
It's just me
Or if anyone
Is coming
Is following
Me, until I see
An interloper
Staring at me
Staring back
Which turns
Out to be just
My reflection
Wide-eyed surprise
Just for a second
Until it turns
And then it's gone
I look around to see
If anyone noticed
The eyes, of course,
But then again,
There's nothing
They don't see
Out here
On the trail

June 16, 2019

The Little Hierophant

Whately, Massachusetts

At the Beals Preserve in Southborough, Massachusetts, they have an annual event called Art On The Trails where they have an art installation along the trails in the woods every summer. This year there are 16 works of art. They invite poets to walk the trails and write poetry based on the art. This is my poem for the art entitled, "What Are?"

June

Empty Kayak

Walking along the trail
I found a seat perched
At the water's edge
So I rested and appreciated
The view that someone
Was thoughtful enough
To place a chair facing.
I looked out and saw
The empty kayak
Floating in the middle
Of this tranquil scene
Surrounded by lily pads.
I sat in the seat
Trying to understand
Reflecting on the deeper meaning
When I started realizing
This was not made for me
Despite the apparent hospitality of it all
This seat
I'm occupying
Is for her
As a private place to come to
As a way
To focus on,
To think about,
To hold onto
What has been lost.
That kayak over there
Is for him
As a place
To visit when he wants
To return,
To enjoy,
To visit,
To be with
Her.
You and I can come here too

The Little Hierophant

To appreciate nature
But most of all
This is a place of learning.
To learn how
To hold onto,
To appreciate,
To love,
The preciousness of life
While we still have it
Here,
Right now,
In this moment

    June 22, 2019
    Whately, Massachusetts

Another poem about a deeply emotional piece of art at the Beals Preserve.

Wishing Circles

Leftover yard sale remnants
Dangling from a series of sticks
Hanging from tree branches
Is this a trap meant to entice
Someone to reach upward
Only for a net to fall down
And ensnare the hapless?
Is it a happy gathering
Of actual wishing circles
For the optimists among us
To make the world better?
Or, is it meant to be
A fancy resting spot
For passing birds?
So many questions
Remain unanswered
For the casual hiker
Who didn't read the sign
For the art in question

    June 22, 2019
    Whately, Massachusetts

Another Beals Preserve poem.

You Are Not Here To Coast

You are not here to coast
If you were
You would not have come back
To this world
To this place
To this life
You are currently inhabiting
So make this go-around
One that's worth it
Make it memorable
Get up
Show up
Be bold
Be brave
Do not give a single fuck
What others may think
Of you
Or what you're doing
Because this life is *yours*,
Not theirs,
So be the best version of you
That you can possibly be
Be the tryhard
Be the overachiever
Be the supernova in the sky
That catches everyone's attention
That they all have no choice but look up to
Because that's you
Up there
Being amazing
Inspiring others
Shrugging off the decades of social pressure
Ignoring the words,
The anger, the jealousy
Moving past failures
Getting up after falling
Again, and again, and again,

June

And forging your own path
Succeeding, achieving your dreams
Like the blazing star that you are
Higher and brighter
Than you ever thought possible
Until you've reached the end
Of your time, this time around,
Taking stock of everything
With a beautifully full life
Under your belt
Richly lived,
And worth being proud of

        June 29, 2019
        Whately, Massachusetts

The concept of this popped into my mind and hit me hard last night. It's like I *just now* realized this. I spend way too much time worrying about what other people may think of what I am, or what I do. That time and energy over the last four and a half decades could have been *much* better spent focused solely on *creating* rather than worrying.

Back A Page

I think I did something good right there
Back a page
But I'm not sure
It's just a feeling I have
Which is not something I should dwell on
Because the past is back there
And I'm here, in the future
Moving on
A little more experienced
Than I was back then
With my head slightly higher
And my smile a little bigger

                June 29, 2019
                Whately, Massachusetts

Sometimes I write without thinking. I blank my mind and let my fingers do the words. This was one such time.

June

Rainbow Wall

Sometimes hope
Is a thing found
Rainbowing down
From up above
To the forest floor
You just have to be
In the right spot
(Like this one here),
At the right time
(Like right now),
To be lucky enough
To see
To experience
The rainbow wall
And feel it
Radiating
Uplifting
Filling you
With joy
And hope

        June 30, 2019
        Whately, Massachusetts

Another poem about a piece of art at the Beals Preserve. This one was chosen for inclusion in their annual poetry collection, *Art On The Trails: Marking Territory*. I also read this at the closing event and poetry walk event on September 22, 2019.

JULY

New Keyboard

These are the very first words written
On my brand new keyboard
Which, for a writer,
Is like a professional driver
Getting behind the wheel
Of a brand new car
It takes a while to learn
Where everything is
The distances involved
And how fast you can comfortably go.
Apart from the oversized function keys
Along the top row
And the extra reach involved
To hit the delete button
With my right pinky
Everything seems to be going pretty well
Much better than my old keyboard
Which decided that I no longer needed
To use the T, G, or B keys
Or the right directional arrow
For that matter
Which is something
I'm just not going to allow
A keyboard to choose for me
So I added it to the pile
Of worn-out keyboards
Making me wonder
If maybe
Just maybe
The problem is me
And I'm the one
Who's a little too rough on them

        July 2, 2019
        Whately, Massachusetts

July

Did you know that you can no longer buy a wired, full-sized keyboard from Apple? That's bonkers. Luckily, I was able to find a nice aluminum one from a different company that looks and feels the same as my old one.

When I said, I added the broken keyboard to the pile, I wasn't kidding. That's the second Apple keyboard that's crapped out on me in the past year.

Although, that reach up to the *delete* key is going to be a toughie.

Mine

Such an offhandedly-simple word
Spoken in a forgettable moment
With a weight lasting
Far too long
With a heaviness hanging
Deep, like a gravity well
In the center of my brain
As she pointed to the headphones
On my head as I wrote
And casually said,
"Mine,"
As she passed through the room
A gentle reminder
That these were hers
And would remain so
In two months
When she drove off
On the day we separated

        July 2, 2019
        Whately, Massachusetts

I guess I'd better find my headphones.

Cloud In My Yard

This time of the year
The sun is up
Way before me
So it's brightfully daylight
When I wake up
After shuffling into the kitchen
I looked over the sink
Into the open acres
Of the backyard
And saw the cloud in my yard
Just sitting right there
Minding its own business
Taking up the whole view
With its puffy grayness
Which is weird
Because out front
The windows showed
Happy radiating sunlight
But back here was
A completely different story
Of quietly shrouded
Contemplativeness
Mutedly obscuring
The normal landmarks
The trees, the chipmunks,
The grass, the rabbits,
Until the sun peeked
Around the corner
Shining its blatant truth
Into the soft discretion
Scaring it
Scattering it
Making it flee
Further into the backyard
Hiding behind the line of trees
Which provided a safe spot
Just for a little while

The Little Hierophant

Until the Sun's rising vantage
Allowed it to sniff out
And scare off
The trespassing cloud
That was here uninvited
But whose presence
I genuinely welcomed

        July 2, 2019
        Whately, Massachusetts

Power Button

A power button
Works both ways
To turn things off
And to turn them on
This one is no different
Other than the materials used
And the impressive size
Which are important
Since it has a big job to do
Because when you come here,
To nature,
You need to turn off
Your electronic devices
You need to unplug
Your attached distractions
In order to appreciate
The world around you
And in doing so
You are turning on
The connected part
Of yourself
That's one with
The natural environment
You came from
So, to activate
The experience
You're about to have
Stand in the center,
Power down your phone
Take out your headphones
Put them away
And turn on your senses
Open your eyes,
Breathe in the freshness,
Reach out and touch nature,
(Except for poison ivy –
 you should leave that alone)

The Little Hierophant

And be present here and now
To fully enjoy
This beautiful place
You are immersed in

        July 6, 2019
        Whately, Massachusetts

Another one for the Beals Preserve! I'm really writing a lot for this project.

I wrote this while listening to "This Must Be The Place" by the Talking Heads on repeat.

July

My Need Is Your Taking

I do not belong here,
In this place,
My home is elsewhere,
Somewhere far away,
Where I must contend
With completely different concerns
Yet, here I am,
Looking out of place
But that's okay
I don't mind
Standing out,
Attracting attention,
Because that's what I do
Why am I here?
Well, you have something
That I want,
That I need
More than anything,
Something precious
That's mine for the taking
And as an invasive species
There is nothing to stop me
Since there are no distractions,
And definitely no competition
As I know the lay of the land
So intimately well
And I am not afraid
To step in and take
What I want
What I need
Which is…

Everything

    July 6, 2019
    Whately, Massachusetts

The Little Hierophant

Another one about an artwork on the trails at the Beals Preserve. I honestly didn't much care for the art itself for this one, but I did like the meaning behind it, highlighting invasive species.

This one was chosen for inclusion in their annual poetry collection, *Art On The Trails: Marking Territory*. I also read this at the closing event and poetry walk event on September 22, 2019.

July

The Moments Of Uncharacteristic Bravery

It's the moments
Of uncharacteristic bravery,
Which define a life
Where you stand up
Not to a person
Or some enemy
But to yourself
And your fears –
Those damnable
Inhibiting fears
That stop you
Dead in your tracks
From doing what you want
From being who you're meant
To be in this life
Stand up to yourself
Stand up for yourself
Be who you want to be
Always.

        July 6, 2019
        Whately, Massachusetts

I Felt Like I Slept Through An Entire Generation

I feel like I slept through
An entire generation
Where all I did was work
Long hours, days, years,
Accomplishing so much
For a giant corporation
In the moment, back then,
Locked firmly in the past
And now I'm waking up
And realizing that *life*
Is so much more
Than working,
Watching TV,
And paying bills –
Leaving nothing much
Behind in my wake
But deep exhaustion
And dreams unfulfilled
As was the practice
For the past decades
Finding myself here
In my mid-forties
With the right mindset
I wish I had in my twenties
So I could have made
Something of myself
Instead of starting over
From scratch, yet again
As I've done before
But this time
I'm going to push through
And do things my way
Working hard and
Trusting my gut
To go where I know
I need to be

July

July 6, 2019
Whately, Massachusetts

I think subconsciously, I just needed to write a poem with a longer title than the last one.

Bouncing Ball

Three seconds
Frozen
Stretched out
So the images
Charting the course
Of the bouncing ball,
Dancing across
The old fence,
Are visible
Like frames
From a film
Where time itself
Has been stopped
Opened, dissected,
Allowing the scene
To be studied
From every angle
So we can understand
The physics of it
Despite not knowing
The elusive answer
To the biggest question
As yet unasked:
How this simple ball
Ended up here, in this spot
In the first place

    July 6, 2019
    Whately, Massachusetts

Yet another poem about an art piece at the Beals Preserve. I think I'm now running out of art I want to write about.

This one was chosen for inclusion in their annual poetry collection, *Art On The Trails: Marking Territory*. I also read this at the closing event and poetry walk event on September 22, 2019.

July

Galaxies Are Stepping Stones

Galaxies are stepping stones
Allowing you to get
Across the universe
From here to where
You're trying to go
Without getting your feet wet

        July 7, 2019
        Whatley, Massachusetts

Five years ago, when I lived in Portland, Oregon, I did a Life Between Lives (LBL) hypnotherapy session with a Newton Institute-trained LBL hypnotherapist in Washington. Last night I was listening to part of my recording from that session and one of the things I said in regards to traveling around the Universe between lives was that, "Galaxies are stepping-stones," and laughed when I expounded by saying, "So you don't get your feet wet." I don't know what it means, but I thought it might make for a neat poem.

The Dude On The Motorcycle

The dude on the motorcycle
Behind me on the highway
With his full-face mirrored visor
Looked like a robot man and
Reminded me that I needed
To download more Daft Punk
To my playlists on Spotify

       July 7, 2019
       Whately, Massachusetts

Today I drove down to Hadley to run some errands. While there, I stopped to Home Depot to get a new window shade for the bedroom. The shades in this house are probably 50 years old and are *very* brittle due to decades of exposure to the sun. Last fall, I gently swatted at a fly on the shade in the bedroom with a book and was surprised when the book went *through* the shade. I've been meaning to replace it for months, and today was the day I finally did it.

I brought the old hole-y shade to Home Depot and the shade guy measured the old one and cut a new shade to the same width. (Note: the window shades at the Home Depot are *not* in the window department. They are, for some unknown reason, in the *flooring* department. I'm not sure why.)

When I got home, I went to put the new shade in…and it was two inches too wide. Come on! I mean, gee whiz. The guy had the old shade to measure and did not take into consideration that he needed to subtract the roll-y bits on the ends from the width.

Anyway, I had to go back to Home Depot to have them re-cut the shade. On the way down there for the second time, I saw this motorcycle in my rear-view mirror. His helmet kinda sorta looked like the helmets the guys from Daft Punk wear, which made me

July

realize that when I started creating playlists in Spotify a few months ago, I neglected to add any Daft Punk songs.

I have since corrected that oversight.

Because Of My Beep

I can't go there
I want to
That's the place
I intended to go
When I left my house
But now I can't
Due to the fact
I honked at someone
Who was fiddling with their phone
Instead of paying attention
To the traffic light
Which turned green
More than several beats too-long ago
And now that car happens to be turning
Into the place I was going to go
So, to avoid a confrontation
Because of my beep,
I continued straight,
To who knows where,
Instead of following
The jerky jerk
Into a situation
That was probably much worse
Playing in my brain
Than it ever would have been
In real life

   July 7, 2019
   Whately, Massachusetts

This did not actually happen, because I refrained from honking my horn at the person, but I imagined how it would have played out.

I guess I *really* am "The Peacemaker" (#9) Enneagram Type Description.

July

I Want To Be A Do-er

I want to be a do-er
But I also
Want to be a don't-er
I want to feel good
At having accomplished
At having finished things
Enjoying the feeling of success
But I also want to relax
And do absolutely nothing
And all that it entails
Enjoying the feeling of sloth
Instead, I find myself
Squarely in the middle
Crawling slowly
Getting stuff done
At a baby's pace

          July 13, 2019
          Whately, Massachusetts

Pringle Fountain

I misheard the lyrics
And I thought she said,
"Pringle fountain,"
Which, of course,
She didn't say
But now I can't stop thinking about it
Because the picture
Of a big stone fountain
Spraying waves of salty chips
Up and out, and all about
Is like a looping .gif file in my brain
And way more interesting
Than what the words actually were

        July 13, 2019
        Whately, Massachusetts

I'm so sorry, Lizzo.

July

The New Car Feel

Nothing beats enjoying
The new car feel
The new car smell
As you push things hard
To test the limits
To see what you can do
Hugging, holding,
Appreciating the curves
Laid out before you
Muscles tightening
As the heart is racing
Nearly as fast as you
As you drive roads
Never before taken
To add to the thrill
On the way to that
Top tourist attraction
Seemingly the
Most visited place
In the entire state
Because, why not
Take a new road
To add to the fun,
The excitement
Of the experience
Breaking things in
While breaking out
Of the routine patterns
With the gloriousness
Of this absolutely perfect
Fucking machine
Taking you where
You want to go –
Anywhere at all

    July 13, 2019
    Whately, Massachusetts

The Little Hierophant

I can't wait to take the new car on Route 2 to go to Mass MoCA and the Clark Art Institute. It's such a curvy, fun, amazingly scenic road to drive on.

July

I Bear Witness

Because I rise with the sun
I bear witness
To the increasing tragedy
Of the shortening light
Experiencing dimly-lit dusk
When a few weeks before
I enjoyed full-on sunshine
And every day going forward
I'll wake to less than now
Until complete darkness
Will eventually become
The standard environment
To which I will awaken

>July 13, 2019
>Whately, Massachusetts

Somehow, it just feels wrong. It's *summer*. The sun should always be up by 4:30 am and not set until 10 pm. Then, after Labor Day, the sun can start rising later, and setting earlier. Not before.

Unknown To Forgotten

Completely unknown
Is the starting place
For nearly everyone
Then the idea hits
And something tangible
Becomes of it
As it finally takes shape
And is finally presented
To an oblivious world
Who does not know
Or care of this new thing
Until someone takes notice
Not many, just a few at first
Who really enjoy it
And tell others why
They would like it too
Word spreads
More people like it
And it starts to become
A real thing
With legs of its own
When the news,
Needing something
On a slow day,
Picks it up and runs with it
Showing the masses
What they're missing out on
Which causes the thing
To go from "HOT!" to "HUGE!"
And the thing is now
Everywhere
You can't escape it
Which is when
The backlash begins
The critical words
Previously just a mild murmur
Found its voice

July

And a megaphone
In those who are sick of it
Or feel they could do better
Or just have never liked it
Which knocks the creator
Down several notches
Just as the fervor
Starts to die down
A coincidence in timing
But it doesn't feel like it
So the creator gets busy
On the next big project
Working hard on building
It from idea to fruition
But, when it's done,
Now there's a team
Helping to market it
Working hard to
To sell the hell out of it
Because money needs money
To make more money
And it doesn't happen on its own
So a polished and professional
Campaign, carefully created,
And artfully designed
Is made to promote the new thing
To talk it up, to create buzz
Leading to the release
Which, eventually arrives
To a flurry of "meh" reviews
Because it wasn't exactly like
The last thing, the first thing,
The thing everyone liked
It was too different
And people don't like things
Which are different
From what they know
And are comfortable with
So, somewhere a boss

The Little Hierophant

Reviewed some numbers
And made a decision
To pull the marketers
To remove the help
To abandon the creator
Because they weren't making
The exact percentage forecasted
Which comes as a huge blow
To the creator, who, by now,
Has gotten used to a level of success
And now is left with nothing
But the creator needs to continue
Because that's what they do
And has found freedom
Doing what they wanted
On their own terms
So they continued doing
What they felt called to do
Never achieving the same
Outrageous level of success
But eventually came to terms
With it and, with therapy,
Is totally fine with it
The years passed
And being recognized in public
Dwindled from "often" to "never"
Which took some getting used to
So did the "Where are they now?"
Clickbait articles online
Written by people who churn out content
Designed for maximum views
That would pop up every few years
More time meant fewer articles
Then, of course, death
Which brought about a tiny resurgence
And a small celebration of the creator
By the giant company as a way
To capitalize on the opportunity
And did so every decade for a while

July

Creating "anniversary" editions
Until no one really cared anymore
Except for the history buffs
Who delved into the obscure
But with the passage of even more time
Eventually, the creator was finally
Completely and totally
Forgotten

>July 14, 2019
>Whately, Massachusetts

I don't really know what specifically prompted me to write this. I was thinking about musicians and how so many of them toil as complete unknowns – but some manage to get noticed…only to be discarded by a fickle public. I guess it's about the life cycle of a creator from being unknown, to being popular, to being forgotten.

Cats Are Conditional

Cats are conditional
Giving their love
Attached with forms,
Complex riders,
And convoluted,
Intricate paperwork
Written in legalese
That must first be
Figured out, interpreted,
And signed in triplicate
Before they'll allow
You the privilege
To scratch their chin
But if you didn't read
Subsection 43F
Paragraph 2
About the timing
And direction
Of the chin scratching
They will cut you
Before you can blink
And leave you bleeding
Where you stand

        July 14, 2019
        Whately, Massachusetts

Or…they're completely relaxed and will let you pose them for all the goofy Instagram pictures you want.

July

Watching The Wind

Watching the wind ripple through
The field way out back
On the sunny, heat-wave day
Making the waist-high greenery
Of the unknown crop
Undulate like the ocean
But considerably less refreshing

>July 21, 2019
>Whately, Massachusetts

I'm not 100% sure what's growing back there. Last year it was a potato field, but the green stalky things seem too tall for that. It looks more like it could be corn. Anyway, it's rippling in the wind.

My Fitbit Is Lowering Its Expectations

Every couple of hours
I feel a brief vibration on my wrist
Most of the time I ignore it
But sometimes I will actually look
And, when I do, it honestly seems that
My Fitbit is lowering its expectations
Because the challenges it offers me
Have noticeably steeply diminished
At first, wanting me to take 300 steps,
When that went unheeded and unnoticed
It tried to bargain with me to try for 90,
Then begging for just a dozen, *that's all*,
Or asking me to fall out of my chair –
It knows I'm still alive, so I can't trick it
Unless I just take it off completely
Which might finally silence it for good

                July 21, 2019
                Whately, Massachusetts

Just kidding!

(Sort of.)

July

The Last Lightning Bug

The last lightning bug
Of the half-done summer
Passed by the other night
I'm not sure where it was
Heading, but at least it
Had its own party light
Of the most vibrant neon
As it blinked blinked by

        July 21, 2019
        Whately, Massachusetts

I think their numbers have dropped sharply. When I was a kid, our backyard was like something out of a dream with thousands of the green-yellow lights flashing, flashing, flashing. I would stare out my window long after bedtime just to watch them.

Last year, I saw maybe a dozen all season.

This year, there's been a few, but not a lot.

I Felt The Universe

When meditating today
I felt the usual energy
Flowing around
Like I normally do
When, all of a sudden
It was like
I found myself strapped
To a surprise rocket
(*Surprise!*)
That launched me upward
While still being aware
That I was connected
To my body on Earth
Like my soul was being stretched
In a completely painless way
It was just something I was aware of
As I rocketed up through the heavens
Beyond simple space
Into a place lighter and further
Than I could have dared to conceptualize
When I realized I had stopped
It was then,
In the briefest mote of an instant,
I felt the Universe
Or, at least a muted corner of it,
And the interconnectedness
Of all things
Feeling, knowing, what it is like
To be Source energy
Flowing through
Connecting everything
In such a pure way
It wasn't the *entire* Universe
Just a flash of a small bit of it
Because, I was still attached
To my very human body
Whose fragile eggshell mind

July

Would have probably melted
Trying to comprehend,
Absorb, or even look at
The connected entirety
Of all of existence
But that glimpse
I did experience
Has left me unusually
Quiet and pensive
Ever since my meditation ended
And I opened my eyes
Only to hear the sad trumpet sound
"Wah-waah-ing" in my mind
Upon seeing the view
Of my cluttered living room
From my couch
Here on Earth

        July 21, 2019
        Whately, Massachusetts

I've always felt that "wah-waah" disappointment upon opening my eyes after a really good meditation filled with lightness, energy, and spending time elsewhere completely. Today, after experiencing that so, so, so brief moment of *being* Source energy – connected to *everything*, well, it was like a symphony of sad trumpets playing instead of the usual one trumpet.

Strata

Here, before us, is a concrete square
Filled with random bits of daily life
Giving us a glimpse of what people
In future civilizations will see of us
Once they've dug deep through the
Layers of strata built up over eons –
And came across what you see now
As they try to figure out our society
Making their oft-wrong assumptions
Based on the trinkets preserved here

>	July 23, 2019
>	Whately, Massachusetts

Another one for the Beals Preserve contest. The art for this was a square section of concrete, maybe three feet by three feet, with a bunch of trinkets stuck in it. I tried to make the poem physically resemble the art.

This one was chosen for inclusion in their annual poetry collection, *Art On The Trails: Marking Territory*. I also read this at the closing event and poetry walk event on September 22, 2019.

July

(a parenthetical poem)

(parenthesis after the words)
(done to dampen the harshness)
(like whispering)
(all lower-cased)
(lessening the volume)
(but still there, suggesting)
(adding to the conversation)
(with a mild intensity)
(because a point is needing)
(to be made)
(to be gotten across)
(but it's still done quietly)
(because we're still being)
(nicely civilized about everything)
(much like a parenthetical poem)

                July 27, 2019
                Whately, Massachusetts

I wanted to write a poem with a whisper.

I SAID I WANTED TO WRITE A POEM WITH A WHISPER!

It's Completely Up To Me

Sitting alone
Thinking about a future
That is now changed
That is now wide open
Trying to decide
If I should be
Scared or elated
By the decisions
That need to be made
It's not like having
Your plans cancelled
For a Saturday night
This is much deeper,
Fuller, and more complete
Soon it'll be just me
Traversing this road
And it's completely
Up to me on the view
That I choose to see
I can either look at it
From a perspective
Of lack and loneliness
And wallow in sadness
Or, see it for what it is:
A chance at something new
An opportunity to explore
And see a world
Full of possibility
And wonder
One hundred percent
On my own terms
Which, sounds
Considerably more appealing

        July 27, 2019
        Whately, Massachusetts

July

Honkin'

The word, "Honkin'"
Never gets paired
With any other word
But, "Big"
Which is a shame
Because I believe
It has more to offer
If we give it a chance

          July 27, 2019
          Whately, Massachusetts

Malaise Of Choice

While you choose
To bask and sauté
In your most recent
Malaise of choice
With vast plans of
Plating and serving
It up as a grand feast
I will instead choose
To step out for a bit
And get drive-thru instead

        July 27, 2019
        Whately, Massachusetts

Recently Kari used the phrase "malaise of choice" recently to describe herself. I thought it was funny and tried to shoehorn it into a poem of some kind.

July

Always Missing

The daylight filtering into the living room
Went from bright and normal as expected
To something gray and muted just as if
Someone had a knob or a dial that changed
The light levels in my house, but instead
It was for all of outside, so I investigated
The source of this unexpected darkness
Looked out over the backyard and there,
Towering above the land, was a dark stack
Of clouds, rumbling like the hangry stomach
Of a hungry god, so I opened my weather app
And watched the weather map in motion
Which showed this localized thunderstorm
Heading in a direction down and away
So its course would narrowly pass me by
Skimming past, just close enough to feel
The quickening wind, to see the gray smudge
Of the deluging torrents falling just a mile away,
And smell the freshness of the oncoming rain
Except that it never comes
Storms are always passing by
But they are always missing
My town, my street, my house
Every single time, I watch the weather maps
And, just as if a tiny weather Moses
Was standing on my roof separating the storms
They always pass by on one side, or the other
I hear and feel the booming thunder
I see the flashes of lightning
But right here, we get nothing
Each and every time
And I don't know why

        July 28, 2019
        Whately, Massachusetts

True story.

Seriously, whenever there's a storm coming, I can see it hanging out right over there, past the back field, but then it just skims on by and hassles another town. Not that I'm complaining, but it is just odd.

July

What Am I Doing Here?

Sitting at my desk
In my government job
Doing work slowly
Less efficiently
Making it last longer
Just like everyone else
Eventually learns to do
When the full-body chill
Hits me hard along with
Million-dollar questions:
What am I doing here?
Why am I doing this?
Ignoring, by-passing
My talent, my calling
Giving up my time,
My precious time,
To shuffle paperwork
When I could be
Expressing my creativity
Living a life in alignment
With my true self
Day-in and day-out –
Instead of being here
In a sick building
Full of stale air
And crushed,
Withered dreams…
It makes me pause
And wonder to myself
"What am I doing here?"

        July 30, 2019
        Northampton, Massachusetts

What I do to earn money now is pretty much the polar opposite of the real me. At least when I was a hotel General Manager I had to wear a dozen different hats and use my creativity to find different solutions to hundreds of problems. Not here.

Maybe the purpose of this job is to show me the contrast between what I am living through versus what I could have if I focused my energy enough.

It's something to think about.

July

Every Day

Doing something
Anything
Every day
Is the key
To everything

        July 30, 2019
        Northampton, Massachusetts

Sometimes I like to follow a longer poem with a wee li'l poem.

Separation

Separation from the
Mundane, from the
Dreadfully daily routine,
And placing yourself
In new situations
Gives your life
That needed contrast
And makes you expand
Into something so much greater,
So far beyond what you were before

          July 30, 2019
          Northampton, Massachusetts

I guess the subject of the "What Am I Doing Here?" poem really had an impact on me.

July

The Little Hierophant

AUGUST

Moments Like This

It's moments like this
Where you're wrapped
In such a positive
Yet tender moment
Coated with a crunchy layer
Of new-found confidence
Where hopes are realized
And dreams are right there
Within easy reach
That affirm
And reaffirm
What you're doing
Is correct
And true
That you're on
The right path
And it's all
Going to be ok
Because yes,
You CAN do this

        August 1, 2019
        Whately, Massachusetts

What I wrote while listening to "The Melody Of A Fallen Tree" by Windsor For The Derby on repeat. It felt like anything was possible.

August

Expressing Creativity

Expressing creativity
Repeatedly, frequently
Is wonderfully liberating
And perfectly amazing

        August 1, 2019
        Northampton, Massachusetts

I like the interplay of the –ing and –y words.

Fully, Completely, Forever And Ever

I received some very bad news today
The kind that makes your heart sink
Like a clogged sink, overflowing,
Covering your floors with gross disgusting
And the first thought I ended up having
Was, "I need to be cheered up,"
But the thing is, I don't need that at all
I need to be working hard
Focusing on making my dreams
A reality, which will clean up this mess
Fully, completely, forever and ever, amen

                    August 1, 2019
                    Northampton, Massachusetts

August

That Iridescent

I don't think
The roast beef
Is supposed to be
That iridescent –
A color which
Isn't indicative
Of its natural state
Which is why
I passed on by

        August 1, 2019
        Northampton, Massachusetts

Ha! I was done with the poem, which ended with "Of its natural state," and for the notes I typed, "Which is why I passed on by." It took a moment for me to realize, "Hey! That belongs up there, in the poem! Not down here in the notes," so up it went.

The Interplay Between

The
Interplay
Between
The two things
I'm watching
Is utterly, stutterly,
Unequivocally fascinating
And is completely
Beyond words
Which is why I
Will stop writing
And will not be
Describing
What I see
Any longer
So I can step
Into the scene
And be fully
Present and enjoy
This moment
So, I'm sorry
But there will be
No more words
After this one
Right
Here

                  August 1, 2019
                  Whately, Massachusetts

Hoover Dam

The engineering needed
To constrain
To hold back
The forces of
The river
Straining to break through
Wanting to be free
But instead it's
Ensconced and
Stuffed uncomfortably
Into tight confines
By the Hoover Dam
Which is truly a marvel
Especially when you're
There, in the flesh,
And can see
And can feel
The power and the pressure
Of the river as it presses
Against its restraints
And you think
That if there was
Something to trigger
Some kind of release
That would let it all out
It would utterly change
Your worldview
Completely
And totally
In the spark of an instant

        August 2, 2019
        Whately, Massachusetts

The Little Hierophant

I have not stood on top of the Hoover Dam, but I did once fly directly over it on a sightseeing airplane. I imagine this is what would be running through my mind if I were there.

I just realized I used "utterly" in two consecutive poems. That was not intentional.

Time Is A Bullet

Time is a bullet
Flying through the air
Shooting at an unknown target
And you are
A tiny, tiny version of yourself
Balancing on top of it
As it blurs on by
While you're trying
So hard to live or be
Normal in any respect
But it's so hard
Going so fast
And knowing
That, at some point,
This ride *will* end
And *you* with it
But you don't know where
And you don't know when
So you do your best
To do what you can
In the time you've got left
Otherwise, you might as well
Walk to the rounded edge
Lose your footing
And just slide off
But you'll never know
How far you'd have gotten
Or where you'd have ended up
Had you chosen to keep riding

              August 2, 2019
              Whately, Massachusetts

Low Row

Why am I
On the low row
Instead of the
High road
How did I
End up here
Somewhere
That's not
Even a road
But it does
Sound like it
Close but still
It's not a road
It's a row
Which is
I guess
Something
Different
Maybe not
Quite as nice
Or fancy
Maybe it's
Not paved
But an upgrade
From a path
And still
Better than
A trail
But not a road
That's what
I want
That's where
I want to be
Is on a road
One higher
Than this
Low row

August

That I seem
To have
Found myself
Traversing
At the moment

        August 7, 2019
        Whately, Massachusetts

A few days a week, I go to the gym at work. One of the weight machines…well, I should actually say, my *favorite* weight machine is something called the "Low Row." I don't know if that's a correct professional designation, or just a proprietary name the weight machine manufacturer made up for it, but the name stuck with me as oddly short, and cutely rhyming. I took note of it and started this poem with absolutely nothing in my mind other than those two words. I wanted to just write something completely off the cuff.

The Little Hierophant

Determination

Determination
Defines the difference
Between doing –
Achieving something,
And becoming nothing

>August 7, 2019
>Northampton, Massachusetts

I'm a little worried about this one because it's too short, too succinct, and too perfect.

Action Is Happening

Feeling like I'm living
So close
Right there
In the touchable distance
Edging adjacent
To something
BIG
But
It's obscured
And I can't tell
If it's a tall mountain
Towering above
Or a cliff looming
High over a deep pit
Dropping down,
All I can feel
Is its gravity
Pulling, leading,
Drawing me
Closer to the mass of it
Because I can't see
What I'm facing
I'm uncertain if I'll be
Climbing or falling
Succeeding or failing
Continuing or dying
I'm not sure
Which I'd rather have
Either way, it's a change
From the quiet plains
Of ordinary existence
I have traveled
Up to this point
Either way,
Action is happening
So I am taking
Steps in the right direction

The Little Hierophant

No matter the outcome

      August 7, 2019
      Whately, Massachusetts

I wrote this while listening to "The Sun" by The Naked And Famous on repeat.

August

It Comes As No Surprise

It's been years now
Suffering through
The dullard's reign
Shooting his mouth off
Indiscriminately
With each day bringing
Something more shocking
So it comes as no surprise
To see the more mindless
The more gullible
Of those among us
Blindly cheering,
Sharing, celebrating,
And putting into practice
The divisionary hate
The missives sent
Dozens of times a day
And it also comes as no surprise
That we all suffer the consequences

    August 7, 2019
    Northampton, Massachusetts

A Grandfather Clock

A grandfather clock
Has no place
In a modern world
Where time
Is fully uniform
And we all
Are used to having it
Within easy reach
On our phones
While the notion
Of having a giant
Piece of furniture
Whose only function
Is to tell the time
And still needs
Daily maintenance
Is a taxing burden
That, these days,
No one wants

        August 11, 2019
        White River Junction, Vermont

Even if someone offered to give me a grandfather clock for free, I would say no way. It's interesting to see things like this, which were once prized possessions, become junk no one wants.

August

The Hot Air Balloon

The hot air balloon
Intruding on this side of the horizon
Silent, except for the occasional
Jittery roaring
Punctuated by the bright dot
Of the fire filling
Keeping the whole thing
Hanging there
Like a colorful light bulb
Against the pale blue backdrop
Of the waning day's sky

> August 11, 2019
> White River Junction, Vermont

This morning in Whately, I saw a hot air balloon that just hung there in the sky about a half-mile away for the longest time. This evening, from my hotel here in White River Junction, I saw two hot air balloons.

I think they're following me.

The Delicate Nuance

From a distance
The delicate nuance
Of the barely perceptible
Change in elevation
Seems trivial
And hardly noticeable
But once there
In the scene itself
The view from here
Is more than enough
To change your mind
To make you a believer
That such a small thing
Can make a real difference
When enjoying the view
From this vantage point

                August 11, 2019
                White River Junction, Vermont

I was driving around and saw the two hot air balloons mentioned in the notes for the previous poem. I was on a hill that was comprised of several parking lots. When I went to the next lower parking lot, the trees were in the way and I couldn't see the balloons. To me, it didn't seem like all that huge of a difference in elevation, but I guess it was just enough. I went up a bit and then I could see the balloons. They were too far away and my pictures looked terrible, but still the tiny increase in height allowed me to see them.

August

One One-Thousandth Of A Percent

Of all the millions and millions of trees
I pass by on my normal route anywhere
I've begun to notice that, within the past week,
A mild dulling, a faint rusting, on the edges
Nothing concerning, nothing overly telling,
The numbers I'm talking about are so small
Maybe one one-thousandth of a percent
Of all the trees I go by are hinting at turning
Are starting the mentioning of something
Coming down the road sometime soon
Where the muffled murmurs
Will increase to careless whispers
Eventually rising to a conversation
Devolving into a screaming din
Where one season silences another
And passes through to a quieter time
Where only the cold blustery wind
Is the one remaining
Is the one standing
With anything noteworthy to say

        August 11, 2019
        White River Junction, Vermont

The Little Hierophant

Trusted To Flush

The urinal in the men's room
In this building, built
In the 1930s,
Was surprising
In its shape
In its size
And that it didn't have
A modern motion-sensing
Auto-flushing unit on it
Because it was
Something solid,
Made to last
From back in the day
When men could be
Trusted to flush

        August 12, 2019
        White River Junction, Vermont

August

Scale Models

A whirlpool in a tub
Spinning, draining,
A hurricane in the ocean
Churning, damaging,
A galaxy in the universe
Doing everything,
All three are
Scale models
All achieving
The same thing
Only in different magnitudes

    August 12, 2019
    White River Junction, Vermont

I could be wrong, but I think I've written about this before (but differently) a few years ago.

The Little Hierophant

I'm Glad She Sat Elsewhere

At the McDonald's having lunch
When a woman walked past
This sparsely-populated
Area of the dining room
And muttered out loud,
"I know what table I'm not
 Sitting anywhere near!"
I looked up to see the scene
Where two well-behaved kids
Sat coloring, while waiting
For their dad who was brining lunch
And thought to myself,
"What's her problem?
 Those kids are great,"
Until it dawned on me
That she could actually be
Referring, somehow, to me
In which case
I'm glad she sat elsewhere

    August 12, 2019
    White River Junction, Vermont

True story!

Well…it's not much of a story, but it's still true.

August

A Daddy Longlegs

While sitting, having lunch
At a fast-food restaurant
I looked out the window
And saw a daddy longlegs
Doing its thing, walking
Across the sidewalk
But heading to the edge
I tried to send it thoughts
A warning not to proceed
Because there's nothing
In that direction at all
But it ignored my pleas
And ventured across
The extremely busy
Lunchtime drive-thru lane
After several near-misses
I lost sight of it,
So I don't know
If it was successful
But I wish it the best
With whatever it's up to

        August 12, 2019
        White River Junction, Vermont

Another true story from McDonald's!

The Little Hierophant

I Want My Days To Mean Something

I want my days to mean something
To carry weight in the grand scheme
Accomplishing my life's goals while
Also supporting a normal existence
Right now, the two are not aligned
The difficulty lies in bridging the gap
Which seems like a thick river wide
But, if I work at it every single day,
Where I am and where I want to be
Slowly get closer, until eventually,
I am there, in the place I dreamed

    August 13, 2019
    White River Junction, Vermont

August

Dear Dave In Baltimore

Dear Dave In Baltimore
Thank you for the email
You so "eloquently" sent
Deeply critical of my poem
Recently featured on
The Writer's Almanac
Whereupon you challenged me
To defend the lengths of my lines
And tell me what I wrote
Is, in fact, not poetry at all –
But instead of responding,
Replying, or engaging
With some stranger on the Internet
I will put this topic
On the lazy Susan of life,
Spin it back around to you,
And ask you to defend
Your use of twelve mistakes
(grammatical, and spelling –
 apparently all used deliberately)
Over the brief span
Of twenty-three words
(an impressive ratio, for sure),
And the bold stroke
Of how you jammed
The several sentences
Of the email's body
Into the subject line
And placed the subject
In the cavernous area
Where the body goes
But please be aware
That I won't read your reply
Since I marked you as spam
And I honestly I don't care

August 17, 2019

The Little Hierophant

Whately, Massachusetts

Gee whiz!

Random people will send the weirdest shit to complete strangers online. I can't imagine what people who are actually famous have to deal with.

It reminds me of that meme of the very angry kid playing chess with the caption, "STOP LIKING WHAT I DON'T LIKE!"

August

Frogs Or Flags

At the counter
At the post office
When the worker
Asked which I wanted
Stamps with frogs or flags
I chose the former
Because they were
Fun, colorful, and different
As he rang me up
He pointed to a drawer
Overfull with flag stamps
And remarked that nobody
Wants the flags anymore

        August 17, 2019
        Whately, Massachusetts

Such Triviality

Why do items
Of such triviality
Occupy so much
Time, space, and energy
In the minds of so many
So, instead of focusing
Our collective thought
On things of importance
We're all too caught up
Stressing about
The lives of idiots

                 August 17, 2019
                 Whately, Massachusetts

August

Disquieted

Pulled into a space
And parked the car
Disquieted
By seeing the car
Next to mine
Rolling forward
Making me think,
For a frantic moment,
I didn't put mine
Into park –
Fearing my car
Was continuing
Toward an accident

        August 17, 2019
        Whately, Massachusetts

This happened in the Dunkin Donuts parking lot in White River Junction yesterday morning. My heart nearly jumped through my chest after I pulled in, looked over and saw the car next to me rolling forward, making me think I didn't put my car into park.

The Purpose

The purpose
For being
Here
Is complex
And layered
Everything
Has a reason
Everything
Has a place
Everything
Has meaning
Everything
Teaches us
Everything
Gives life lessons
Seeing how they fit
Like puzzle pieces
Seemingly chaotically
Oftentimes painfully
Apparently without reason
Dropping from the sky
Upon us like anvils
But then
With perspective
Watching them all
Fall into place
So neatly, perfectly,
Gives me the chills
To watch
As everything
Happens
Just as it should

        August 18, 2019
        White River Junction, Vermont

August

I wrote this while listening to "Anything You Synthesize" by The American Dollar on repeat.

Feeling The Connection

Feeling the connection
The deeply rooted link
The upwelling energy
From the Earth below
And the Universe above
Both grounds and uplifts me
Strengthening and connecting
The soul I am
Between the two

        August 18, 2019
        White River Junction, Vermont

I just meditated for the first time in about a week. It was ok, probably a B- overall, but the energy has really stayed with me long after finishing. I feel like I'm wearing a big heavy winter coat or a snowsuit covering my whole body made of pure energy that is radiating off of me, but is also lighter than air.

One of the things that came to me during this meditation was that I needed to connect more with the spiritual side of myself and to not give any thought to what others may think about it. So, here I am, dong just that.

August

Gut Reaction

From now on
I'm going to go
With my gut reaction
Instead of my
Analytical mind
Because I have
The terrible tendency
To overthink
And second-guess
And third-guess
And tenth-guess
And so on
When, it turns out
That my natural instinct
Was right all along

        August 18, 2019
        White River Junction, Vermont

Steady Hearty Breeze

The steady hearty breeze
Tinged with coolness
Nothing approaching a freeze
But a real awareness
That the seasons are changing
Despite our lack of permission

        August 25, 2019
        Whately, Massachusetts

August

Stalled

I feel like I've stalled
I've completely stopped
In every respect
And while I know how
To get going again:
Just put one foot
In front of the other
Just do something, anything
And do it every day
Until I'm somewhere else,
I don't know the direction
Because my compass
Is overwhelmed
And frustrated
As it's both spinning furiously
And not showing anything
Tangible, usable, helpful
And the worst part is
My own guidance system,
My gut in which
I've always placed my trust,
Is shrugging with uncertainty –
I know what I don't want
And, I guess, that's what
Is helping me to move forward
Is pushing me away from
All of the stuff not resonating
With my vibrational alignment

                August 25, 2019
                Whately, Massachusetts

The Screen Saver Factory

Here I am
In the place
The flawless place
Where everywhere
I point my camera
Is picture-perfect
Where everywhere
I turn to look
Is nothing but
Unabashed perfection
From fog-caped mountains
To dream-like turquoise waters
Where I have to
Actually restrain myself
From posting photos
Of everything I see
To Instagram
Because everyone
Will think I'm too braggy
About being here
In the screen saver factory

    August 25, 2019
    Whately, Massachusetts

One of Kari's best friends is in Bali and described it as a "screen saver factory." Sorry, Emily, but I needed to run with that line. Thank you!

A Well-Sculpted Topiary

I've gone ahead and done it
I made the decision and now
I'm the end of the line –
Me, me, me, me, me, me,
As I took my pruning sheers
And turned my family tree
Into a well-sculpted topiary
Ensuring nothing,
Ensuring no one will come
After me, after I am gone,
Only the words
And the collected books
I have left behind,
I have planted in my garden
Keeping the topiary company
In the different kind of a family
I have opted to leave as my legacy

    August 25, 2019
    Whately, Massachusetts

I got a vasectomy on Friday.

The Dulling

The dulling is now in full swing
The sunlight isn't as harshly bright
The nights are downright chilly
The geese are all heading south
And we are left with the remnants
Of what remains of the summer
The well picked-over bits
No one wanted because they are
Either dreaming of what was, or
Looking forward to what's to come

        August 26, 2019
        Whately, Massachusetts

August

The Little Hierophant

SEPTEMBER

Summer Is Over Today

Summer is over today
But some may say
Summer's not over
Until after Labor Day
Others will declare
It's still summer until
The autumnal equinox
In much later September
While parents affirm
Summer's totally over
When all of the kids
Are back in the classroom
But in honest reality
We all agree with me
In saying definitively
Summer is over today

    September 1, 2019
    Whately, Massachusetts

September

$7.11

I was being rung up
At the local Circle K
When my total came to
$7.11
Which seemed wrong
Or, at the very least,
More appropriate
For a different store
Where such an amount
Would be welcome
As a convenient coincidence

           September 1, 2019
           Whately, Massachusetts

True story.

The Slow Let-Go

Things are no longer
Heading upward
Or even on a level
They were at one point
Until gravity became
Too strong
Undermining
Diminishing
Disintegrating
Forcing the declination
To the point
Where now
It's noticeable
Where now things
Are curving in a
Downward trajectory
Spiraling, approaching
The inevitable…
The slow let-go

        September 1, 2019
        Whately, Massachusetts

September

Fortune I had Taped Over

Here I was
Thinking about how
I can't seem to get
Anything done
That the act of completion
Seems beyond my grasp
In regards to the things
I want, I need to accomplish
In this lifetime
When I looked up
At the fortune cookie fortune
I had taped over
My computer's camera
Years ago when I first got it
And then promptly forgot about
The fortune telling me
"You should be able to undertake
 and complete anything."
Surrounded by a smiley face
On either end of the sentence
And now it seems so simple
As it was there all along
Just staring me in the face
All I had to do was look up
For the inspiration I required
To know that
All that's needed
Is for me to
Dig in
And
Get it
Done

September 2, 2019
Whately, Massachusetts

The Little Hierophant

With American Eyes

I cut open the package
And spilled the contents
Onto the cookie sheet
And spread the fries
Into a single layer
But I paused
And looked
Thinking it wasn't enough
For the two of us
Until I consulted
The empty bag
And saw it was
(with surprise)
One full pound
Of French fries
Meaning that the
Half pound each
Didn't seem enough
When looked at
With American eyes

        September 3, 2019
        Whately, Massachusetts

True story…which is indicative of a wider problem.

(No pun intended.)

Caught In Pause

I live for and love
Seeing glimpses of
Average moments
Caught in pause
Giving a dramatic
Album cover feel
The kind of look
Defining a sound
More succinctly
Than I ever could

>September 3, 2019
>Whately, Massachusetts

Originally, I had written just the middle part:

>*Average moments*
>*Caught in pause*
>*Giving a dramatic*
>*Album cover feel*

And almost left it at that thinking it was pretty darn good. Short, but good. After staring at it for a long while, I came up with the other lines while listening to the nearly 11-minute song, "Pass The Hatchet, I Think I'm Goodkind" by Yo La Tengo.

Giggle Her

Giggle her
At something funny I said

Giggle stranger
Sitting at the table next to us
At something unrelated
Causing her to be taken aback
Thinking he was laughing at her

Giggle me
At seeing this little laugh echo scenario

        September 5, 2019
        Whately, Massachusetts

Last night at Riff's in Turners Falls. Massachusetts.

September

Luckily It's Only A Half Moon

I hope the neighbor's house
Is strong enough
To support the weight
Of the Moon
Sitting on top of it
Perched while tipped
Low to the horizon
Like an orange wedge
Hanging out on their house
While they are blissfully unaware
Of what's going on up there
Because the Moon is quiet
And grinning at just me
Who is looking at this and thinking,
Luckily it's only a half moon
Because if it was the whole thing
Their nightly TV watching
Would get a rude awakening
Of a planetoid falling through –
Squishing them thoroughly

           September 5, 2019
           Whately, Massachusetts

The Red Leaf

Walking in my yard
When a spot of color
Snagged my sight
A bright dot of red
In a sea of green
And as I got closer
I saw the red leaf
Sitting so vibrantly
Which made me
Look all around
Trying to see if
A tree had suddenly
Changed overnight
The answer was no
Everything was green
Same with the other trees
In all of the yards nearby
Meaning this little guy
Had either flown here
By means unknown
Or, well, I don't know
Maybe it got a ride
From an Uber somehow
Leaves are mysterious
And I do not profess
To understand their ways

    September 7, 2019
    Whately, Massachusetts

I saw this leaf while walking Baxter, just now.

September

The Sad Shame Of A Society

The sad shame of a society
Where there are those among us
Who openly hate
Or actively try
To marginalize others
On the basis of
Their appearances,
Private predilections,
Or perceived origins,
And want to divide
And separate the fabric
Holding us together
Forcing us to bend and break to
Accommodate their ill-founded,
Irrational, racist, xenophobic fears

Which is why we all need
To fight as hard as we can
To resist this hate
To call out the bullying
To tell them this will
NOT be tolerated
And to be working
To bridge differences
And bring us ALL closer
Into a more unified whole
In a much better world
With a brighter future

        September 7, 2019
        Whately, Massachusetts

I recently came across a social media page of a friend of a friend who was extremely blatant and excessively proud of their contrarian views, which seem to be a means of just getting a rise out of others. Maybe they actually believe the manufactured talking points they're parroting, but it's just so sad to see people behaving in this way toward other human beings.

September

Parroting

The loud
Grating
Annoying
Irritating
Squawking
Coming
From those
Parroting
The talking points
Made by the cunning few
Manufacturing the news
Is creating a racket
Making it hard to hear
The voice of actual reason
Whispering rationally from
Our collective conscience

        September 7, 2019
        Whately, Massachusetts

I was inspired by the term "parroting" from the notes of my last poem.

Letting The Words Blur

Staring at the screen
Letting the words blur
Into little black blobs
On a background
Of bright white
The mind realizes
That there is more
Than the up and down
Ebbing of cyclical life
That you can arrow through
Horizontally across the scene
By-passing the drudgery completely
Or, for something completely new,
Choose to pierce the boundaries
Of the dimensional space
Beyond anything ever known
Darklining through the doorway
Between the sub-atomic particles
Where existence is just energetic
Just like us, when you get past
All of the visible density
Comprising the touchable view,
And begin to comprehend
The fascinating vastness
Of everything that is

        September 7, 2019
        Whately, Massachusetts

I was staring blankly at a Word document and my eyes went out of focus. As the words blurred in front of me, the entirety of this poem jammed instantly into my head.

Note: the term "darklining" is a word I made up for my science fiction novel *2492*. Basically, it's how they achieve faster than light travel by piercing through the fabric of space-time and

September

tapping into the dark energy that comprises the bulk of the Universe.

While writing this, I listened to "Someone Great" by LCD Soundsystem on repeat.

The Energy Of The Moment

What I most remember
About the life selection room
After making the choice
To return to this planet
Is the energy of the moment
The childlike anticipation
Of a kid seconds before
Being unleashed on
A massive pile of presents
So intensely excited
So wanting to get back
To Earth, and get back
Into the game,
Into another life,
One with so much potential
Into THIS life
SO MUCH SO
Like I *knew* just what to do
This time around
And I could not wait
To get back into it
That I felt just like
A cartoon character
Whose body stood in place
While their legs spun like a blur
Until they caught purchase
And zipped away instantly
To this amazing opportunity –
The life I'm currently living

        September 9, 2019
        Whately, Massachusetts

I've been thinking a lot about LBL (Life Between Lives hypnotherapy) stuff lately. The moment just before I came back was kind of how I feel when I'm playing the online game I play every night called Team Fortress 2. After you die in the game, you hang out watching the game continuing for about 14 seconds. When that time is up, you re-appear in the spawn room and get going on your next life. As the countdown timer is reading *five…four…three…* I get so excited because I *know* what I'll do differently this time around and I can't wait to get back into the game. Returning back to this life was just like that…only a million times more intense.

Melted With The Knowing

Now that I know
What we are and
What lies ahead
The fear of death
Is completely
And utterly
Gone
Melted with the knowing
That it's all absolutely ok
Because we've done this
Hundreds of times before
And keep growing as souls
With each new pass-through

                September 9, 2019
                Whately, Massachusetts

September

Mini-Mercury

The overly loud man
Unabashedly boastful
Filling the space
With his oversized personality
Emotionally elbowing
His way through all of us
Unaware and uncaring
Of how we were
Before his arrival
Cutting in line
Demanding all attention
To be centered solely
On his little mini-Mercury
Acting as if he were a Jupiter
Bulldozing everyone
In the solar system
Through his words
And jarring actions
Because long ago
He learned how to get
Whatever he wanted
And all he had to do
Was not care
About anyone else

>September 20, 2019
>Whately, Massachusetts

I can't believe how people act in public. Geez.

Maybe it should have been a mini-Deimos, because, damn, that moon around Mars is *tiny*.

Long Shadows

Long shadows in the morning
Feel fresh and full
With the promise of a new day
Like anything is possible
Long shadows in the evening
Feel sad and empty
A day devoid of achievement
Saying, "Better luck tomorrow"

    September 20, 2019
    Whatley, Massachusetts

I prefer the morning shadows, but I often find myself surrounded by the evening ones.

September

Brilliant Highlights

Fall colors right now
Are like brilliant highlights
Streaking brazenly
Through the trees
Singing loudly
Making you notice
They're rare
But when you see them
They are *there*
Because there's no way
You could un-see them
And now you know
That autumn is coming

              September 20, 2019
              Whately, Massachusetts

Dresses Are Made To Come Off

Despite how well they are made, or fit,
Never minding the label sewn on the inside,
Or how classy they're supposed to be
The simple fact of the matter is
Dresses are made to come off
So unfasten, unhook, unzip,
And let gravity do the dirty work
Freeing you completely for me

        September 20, 2019
        Whately, Massachusetts

When I'm leaving the pets alone for a few hours or more, I like to turn on the radio for them. The station that comes in best is full of top hit dance/pop songs. The other day when I got home, I was trying to get settled and was vaguely aware that the song on the radio said something like, "Dresses are made to come off." I'm 99% sure I misheard that lyric, but I thought it might be fun to try to write something in the style of a mildly dirty dance song.

September

The Doorway Of Expression

The doorway of expression
Is painted with poetry
Furthering communication
With the art of the mind
Fostering your expansion
Every time you pass through
To make a new creation

        September 26, 2019
        Whately, Massachusetts

Fluffy Cloud, Solid Chunk

Fluffy cloud,
Solid chunk
Both are cats
In distinctly
Different forms
One is like steel
In firmness and density
One is like fog
In puff and spread-ability
Neither likes the other
Which is not surprising
Considering their
Natural opposability

        September 26, 2019
        Whately, Massachusetts

Bunny (the fluffy cloud) and Scooter (the solid chunk).

September

Energy Is Elastic

Feeling the connection
Still binding us together
Over the distance
So many miles
So much time
Wedged between
Separating us
But…
Energy is elastic
And can stretch
To where it needs to go
No matter where we go
It's there – connecting
Bridging our souls
Through each reiteration
On this planet and beyond

        September 26, 2019
        Whately, Massachusetts

Sometimes I just quiet my mind completely, open myself up, and write without thinking about the content at all. I'm not sure what it's about or what prompted it, but here it is.

Passivity

This morning
While on my daily drive into work
An epiphany hit me
Hard
The stark realization
That lately, I've been a passenger
In my own life
Riding in the back seat
Admiring the view
As someone else
Was worried about
The details,
The direction,
And the where –
As someone else drove
While I was, more or less,
Along for the ride
And enjoying the scenery,
Of course,
But the awareness
I felt this morning
Shook me deeply
Because I never saw myself
Being held captive
By my own passivity
But here I am
In that exact situation
Whose solution
Is exceedingly simple:
All I need to do is drive –
I can go wherever I want
Whenever I want
And the only limit
Is my ceaseless imagination

September 27, 2019
Whately, Massachusetts

September

The toughest things to understand are often the most simple.

Every Poem Is A Brick

Every poem is a brick
In the structure I am building
Each one with the potential
To last long after I am gone
What the whole thing will look like
Depends on how often I write
And how I'm putting it all together
Will it be jumbled chaos?
Just heaps of randomness?
Or a castle of some kind?
With organization and beauty?
Hopefully it'll be something
That'll be featured somewhere
Like *Architectural Digest*
And not *Hot Mess Monthly*
Because this is what
I seem to be doing with my life
And it would be nice to think
That I am actually leaving
Something of value
That people can appreciate
Somewhere down the road

        September 27, 2019
        Whately, Massachusetts

Oh wow, I'm really curious to see what *Hot Mess Monthly* would look like now. I have piqued my own curiosity.

September

Foliage Delivery

A week ago I was going to write
About how fall
Was further creeping up on us
With little splashes of color
Here and there
But now I have to throw out that idea
Because I the past few days
Everything has changed
It's like the foliage delivery
Finally arrived
And instead of being
A gradual shift
It's like nature went crazy
With their color palate
And paint sprayers
On every tree in the area
Until we all knew
Without a doubt
That autumn was here

        September 28, 2019
        Whately, Massachusetts

Mouse Pad

I think
This big cat
Has it all wrong
Because it's actually
Called a mouse pad
Something which
He has claimed
As his own
Leaving
No room
For my mouse
On this cat pad

                    September 28, 2019
                    Whately, Massachusetts

Which is difficult when I'm trying to use the computer.

September

Sweet Caressing Silence

Sometimes I just like the quiet
Not having to hear anyone speak
Because when someone talks
There is an expectation
That you have to listen,
Think about what they're saying
And provide a response
Agreeing with their point of view
And articulating it in a way
To further the conversation
Which, when prolonged,
Is draining with inundation
Of too much information
Making me withdrawn
And want nothing but
Sweet caressing silence

    September 28, 2019
    Whately, Massachusetts

True fact: A lot of my favorite music lately is from bands without singers or lyrics.

Another true fact: I don't know the words to most of my favorite songs.

The Little Hierophant

OCTOBER

Good Citizens

The job of those
Paid to lobby
Our politicians
Is to unabashedly
Demonize or destroy
Anything that threatens
To lessen the dual grip
Around the throats
Of the resources
To be exploited
And the profits
To be made
All to ensure
That we are good citizens
And we keep consuming
Whatever they are making

                October 1, 2019
                Whately, Massachusetts

October

Shorting The Future Of Time

Feeling the rising
Behind the knowing
Determining the cause
Of the increasing anger
With those preserving
The old ways of doing
The things, like chasing
Money while shorting
The future of time
Causing untold distress
Upon every one of us
Starting generations ago
Running forever forward
To the dystopian setting
We are awakening to
Deeper every morning
All the while wondering
How dare they
Condemn their children
To a world worse off
Than they received it
How dare they

        October 1, 2019
        Whately, Massachusetts

Thank you Greta for saying what needed to be said last week.

The Sin Is Rising

In unison with the climbing
Of the morning sun
The sin is rising higher
In the post-dawn sky
Making this place
Much more interesting
Than it was just yesterday

                October 1, 2019
                Whately, Massachusetts

October

The Stark Loss Of Contrast

Sometimes just knowing the answer
Can be troubling in a way
Not equipped to handle the assurance
Because the plans you meticulously laid
Have been unceremoniously tossed
Out the window onto the muddy street
And run over by a big truck of coincidence
That the things you wanted more than life itself
Are revealed to be not what you wanted at all
The stark loss of contrast removing the shadows
Which shrouded the simplicity
In the soft, comforting folds of naivety
Showing nothing but the glaring reality
You refused to acknowledge for so long
But there it is –
And now everything has changed

    October 1, 2019
    Whately, Massachusetts

The four poems I wrote tonight were done with zero preparation or advanced knowing. I simply put on my own Poetry Mix on Spotify, sat before an empty Word document, and wrote.

Feeling The Echoing Glimmer

Feeling the echoing glimmer
Emanating from your soul
The one laid bare before me
The one that's mirroring mine
Both calling out to each other
Like two halves forming a whole
Because we are now together
Finally, after too much time
Our yearning searching and
Too many lives spent apart
Our wanting turns to hunger

           October 4, 2019
           Whately, Massachusetts

I sat down without any ideas of what to write and "#1 Crush" by Garbage came onto my playlist, so I just started typing to the feeling of the song.

October

I Feel Like I Could Be

Sometimes when I'm listening to music
That sounds basic and overly simplistic
I feel like I could be a musician
Writing popular songs
That are fun, poppy, different
That people would actually enjoy
But then the reality sets in
Telling me I don't know how to read music
That I have no rhythm or skill
That I don't know how to play any instruments
So I end up giving up the idea
Because making music just for me
Seems like such a silly idea

Sometimes when I'm looking at art
That looks like something I could make
I feel like I could be an artist
Making modern paintings
Of just blobs of color on canvas
Or creating sculptures
Made out of my recycling
Until I realize that I just don't
Have the connections
To get something I could potentially make
Into a gallery or a museum
So I end up giving up the idea
Because making art just for me
Seems like such a strange idea

But here I am, writing poetry
Nearly every day of the year
Publishing voluminous collections
Consistently every single year
And who do I do this for?
Clearly not the money or the fame
I do it for
No one but me

The Little Hierophant

So, why don't I apply this line of reasoning
To other forms of creative expression?
Maybe, if I did, I could transform things
Change "I feel like I could be,"
To "I am."

        October 4, 2019
        Whately, Massachusetts

This poem was written while a cat draped himself awkwardly across the keyboard.

October

My Tiny Corner

I can't be responsible
For the problems
Experienced by other people
I can't let the stress
Of the daily news
Get into my heart
Because it will hurt
To the breaking point
If I try to take it all on
Which I just can't do
I can make sure my part
In my tiny corner
Of this big planet
Is in vibrational alignment
And maybe
Hopefully
It will spread from there

        October 5, 2019
        Whately, Massachusetts

I used to read the news obsessively and I found myself so stressed and upset by everything. I've really cut back on it and I feel a lot lighter and freer now.

Personification

Personification
Of the unforeseen thing
Making the situation
Unexpectedly wacky
For everyone involved

        October 5, 2019
        Whately, Massachusetts

Today, for some reason, I got to thinking about the comments someone from a writers group gave me after reading my science fiction novel, *2492*. He said the cover (showing a planet and space) made him think it was a hard science fiction novel (typically serious in tone and the science is exact – not much made up), but he described the story itself as being "so wacky, just like *The Hitchhikers Guide To The Galaxy,*" and felt there was too much of a disconnect there for him to enjoy the book. His comments annoyed me because they were so way off-base. The book is neither hard sci-fi, or wacky like *Hitchhikers*. It's a regular story about people and it mirrors real life (500 years in the future – in space) showing a little bit of everything; happy times, sad/bad times, with some action thrown in. Nothing zany at all.

That being said, I was thinking today about how the plots of those absurdist-type stories go, which led me to write this poem. Kind of like writing this whole backstory explanation about a tiny five-line poem.

October

Hue Of Blue

Sometimes the sky
Is such a cloudless
Deeply perfect
Effortlessly rich
Hue of blue
That I wonder what
The ocean does
To curb its jealousy
Because the two
Are stuck staring
At one another
For all of eternity
Unless, of course
It happens to be cloudy
On those days the ocean
Is most likely
Secretly very happy

          October 5, 2019
          Whately, Massachusetts

Lately I've been trying to challenge myself by getting a little more rhymey with my poems.

My Job As A Poet

My job as a poet
Is to observe and report
On most everything I see
Which tends to be
An interesting combination
Of the continual cyclical
Nature of Nature
Blended with
The unexpected reflections
Of the human experience
Sometimes it tastes great
And is just what you want
Other times it's a real mess
Just like life
And that's okay
Because existence isn't perfect

            October 5, 2019
            Whately, Massachusetts

Peeking At The Peak

Peeking at the peak
The foliage radiating
Today's the top day
For looking at leaves
Coloring the scenery
Surrounding me now
And after today it all
Will be waning quickly
As the quality and quantity
Start fading and thinning
Until, in a few weeks,
The dazzling memories
Are all that's remaining

              October 13, 2019
              Whately, Massachusetts

The Changeover

The changeover
Happened so slowly
Barely perceptible
Until the color
Unexpectedly sparked
Caught fire
And spread
Like an inferno,
Or a timely meme,
And now it's
Set the countryside alight
Giving such delight
To photo-based
Social media apps
Where the photos
Oversaturated well-beyond
Anything nature would ever do
In a shameless attempt
To get the most likes
And, in the process,
Making reality
And its beauty
Seem boring, dull,
And pedestrian
In contrast

            October 13, 2019
            Whately, Massachusetts

October

Mid-October Killed It All

Maybe it was the storm
That blew through town
Just a few nights ago
Maybe it's the time of year
When this sort of thing
Always seems to happen
But I'm finding myself
Looking for the beauty
That once surrounded me
Up above and all around
Which has been replaced
By the skeletons of trees
Standing uncaring over
The crisp new carpets
Installed overnight
Blanketing and blowing
Spreading their colors
Into every possible corner
All the while I've been
Gathering evidence
Trying to figure out
Who the murderer was
And, just like that,
I had the answer
Mid-October killed it all
Like it did last year
And will again
Over and over
Reliving its serial routine
Again and again, forever

        October 18, 2019
        Whately, Massachusetts

The Color Came Down

Yesterday, the world
Was awash with beauty
Autumnal impressionism
Bursting with brilliance
With every hill astounding
Every stream a painting
Each tree more amazing
Every field screaming
Unfettered perfection
Absolutely everywhere
Like the entire region
Dressed to impress in its
New Englandy finest
Like it hasn't done
For decades, at least
Then, the winds rolled in
Completely fucking it up
And the color came down

>October 18, 2019
>Whately, Massachusetts

Stupid nor'easter.

October

More Coverage

Buttless johnnies
Like assless chaps
But more coverage
Despite the mishaps

>October 18, 2019
>Whately, Massachusetts

My mom was in the hospital recently, and apparently this is what I got out of it.

I'm actually proud of the "buttless"…"but more" bit.

The Little Hierophant

Warmth, Beauty, Fries, And Frosties

It's that time of year
When anything outside
Seems to shut down
From the food carts
To the ice cream stands
All the places I liked
Are closing and gone
Shuttered and done
Finished for the season
Along with the leaves
They're shutting down
From now to the spring
We have to go without
Warmth, beauty,
Fries, and frosties
Making the next six months
Even that much more
Darker and sadder

        October 20, 2019
        Whatley, Massachusetts

I saw on Facebook that the Local Burgy food cart in Williamsburg, Massachusetts is closing today for the season. Yesterday I drove by the farm stand/ice cream place about two miles away from me (whose name I can never remember) and it was *closed* with the barn shut and picnic tables leaning up against it. I also saw the same at Sugarloaf Frostee. The season is over. It's now time for the snow to come and bury us for months.

My Duty

It's my duty
To describe the now
To depict
The beauty
I experience
All around me
To heat it, plate it,
And serve it to you
So you can eat it
And let it fill you
With the energy
Of something new
Showing you a tiny
Speck of my Universe

          October 20, 2019
          Whately, Massachusetts

Wherever It Takes Me

Having a direction in mind
When I previously had none
Feels so stabilizing so grounding
Compared to doing nothing
But spinning around in place
Wishing, hoping, I had something
To focus on, to pin those hopes on
And now I do, so off I go
Onward to wherever it takes me
And no matter where that is
You can be assured it will be
Full of adventure and fascinating

        October 23, 2019
        Whately, Massachusetts

Recently I made a big decision in regards to the direction of my life. Let's see where it takes me.

October

The Past Forgotten

Spending a solid hour
Getting lost deep down
That rabbit hole of remembrance
Looking at Facebook profiles
Of people I haven't seen
In more than a quarter-century
All those lives I used to know
In what seems like lifetimes ago
All those people I wondered about
Where did they go?
What happened to them?
Well, now I know
And, to be honest,
My feelings are mixed
Because the past forgotten
Can be a deeply complex place
When the memories come back
And combine with what I now know

        October 23, 2019
        Whately, Massachusetts

The short answer to the question never asked: we are all works in progress.

This is what happens when I listen to "Windowsill" by Arcade Fire back to back with "September Girl" by Jupiter Sunrise.

The Short Answer To The Question Never Asked

The short answer
To the question never asked
Is that we are all
Works in progress
You
Me
Everyone you see
All of us are working on it
Some of us fail
And that's okay
Some of us succeed for a time
And that's okay
Most of us fall somewhere in-between
And that's okay too
We're all human
Doing what we can
And that's okay

                    October 23, 2019
                    Whately, Massachusetts

This completely sprung from the notes on my last poem.

October

To See A Flower

To see a flower
And admire its color
Shining brilliantly
Like holiday lights
Twinkling for all to see
To get down on the ground
Put your face right in it
And admire its complexity
The patterns, the brilliance
The amazing beauty it has

To hold a flower
And feel its soft velvetiness
As well as the frail delicateness
And understand it's just here
For such a short time
Feeling lucky to appreciate
Such perfection in a tiny thing

To smell a flower
And know that beauty
Takes more forms
Than what can be seen
To experience the power
That attaches to memory
Forever instantly transporting
You to this moment in time

To hear a flower
Honestly, if you can hear a flower
I would recommend running away
Because it's probably angry bees

To taste a flower
Eeeew, gross
Don't do that
Because it's nasty

The Little Hierophant

And you've clearly forgotten
About the bees

      October 23, 2019
      Whately, Massachusetts

Kari is in Portland, Oregon right now. This afternoon she texted me lots of pictures of flowers, (mostly roses) she saw everywhere. That got me thinking about flowers…which turned into this poem.

October

Trusting The Clouds

Early on a Sunday morning
I looked out the kitchen window
And saw such a glorious scene
As the sun had poked a hole
Through the solid bank of clouds
Somewhere back behind me
But I benefitted from the view
Igniting the entire world with color
With what reluctant leaves are left
Clinging to the trees for dear life
Highlighted with such perfect light
Bright and vibrant oranges and reds
Oversaturated and glowing neon-like
Contrasted ideally to the blue-gray
Smoothed-over mass of clouds
Providing the canvas for the picture
That nature was begging me to take
Each of the elements had been lined up
For me to go outside and click away
And, thirty seconds later, I did just that
Only to find the color was already fading fast
As my astral light source was throttled
By the annoyed clouds who only wanted
Their own brand of gray-day uniformity
And the perfect picture I had seen right there
Had been dulled down into such a scene
That no one would want to photograph
Or, for that matter, even look at
Making me regret not acting in the moment
And taking the picture when I saw it
Instead of trusting that the clouds
Would continue to cooperate
For a few moments longer
Which, as I have just found out
Is actually against their nature

October 27, 2019

The Little Hierophant

Whately, Massachusetts

This happened just now. I was in the middle of feeding the pets when I looked up and saw the trees in the backyard go from dull to gloriously lit up right before my eyes. Wow, it looked amazing and I thought to myself that I needed to go outside and get a picture of that. About a minute later, I did go out, and held up my phone to take a picture, but did a double take as the vibrancy that was just there a few seconds ago was gone, and the light was fading fast. Crap.

I wrote this while listening to Murray A. Lightburn's song "Changed My Ways" on repeat.

October

Cursed

The expression of ideas
Is the foremost need
To people cursed with
Excessive creativity

        October 27, 2019
        Whately, Massachusetts

It's not a curse, but sometimes it can be a bit much knowing I have more ideas for things (books, stories, etc) than I'll ever use within my lifetime, and the flow of new ideas never ceases.

One In A Million

At this moment
Being one in a million
Means there's a total of
Seven thousand
Seven hundred
Of you out there
Which is enough to fill
A small friendly town
With the same version
Of the original individual
You think you are

    October 27, 2019
    Whately, Massachusetts

October

The Unequivocal Reassurance

Riding the glowing feeling
Emanating from my being
Radiating fiercely off of me
Causing chills puckering
My entire self, this being
Energetically emitting
The comforting knowing
The unequivocal reassurance
That everything is all right
Completely and totally
Perfectly amazing
And to not worry
About anything
Ever again

                    October 30, 2019
                    Whately, Massachusetts

Faded Beauty

The well-past peak
Fall foliage is
Faded beauty
Like an
Aging movie
Star –
Sure,
It's not as vibrant
And not
What it used to be,
But
It can still catch
Your eye
So effortlessly
So easily
And there's
Something
In that
Which is
More appealing
More mature
Than the flashy spectacle
We had the other week

                October 30, 2019
                Whately, Massachusetts

October

The Unseen Forces

Sometimes the wishing
Becomes something more akin
To relying on the unseen
Forces, mechanisms
That run everything we know
In ways we might not have
Planned, anticipated
But things turn out great
And even better
Than what was wished
To begin with

        October 31, 2019
        Whately, Massachusetts

I wiped my mind completely blank and just typed.

Watching The Cornfield

It has been fascinating
Watching the cornfield out back
Transitioning from
Green, vibrant, tall, thick, and strong
Fading to
Copper, muted, dwindling, reedy, and frail
Dying to
Khaki, pallid, shrunken, sparse, and dead
All over the brief space
Of only a few weeks
Making me regret
Not going back there
And picking some ears
Before it all went away

                    October 31, 2019
                    Whately, Massachusetts

October

The Only Thing I Know

There used to be a time
When everything seemed
Fresh, new and exciting
But somewhere along the way
The color and the joy
Diminished, faded,
The youthful exuberance
The excitement
The ability to count on traditions
And to enjoy and look forward
To what you've always known
Had been replaced
With uncertainty
With feeling like you're on the edge
Of the utter and complete unknown
You're losing your footing
While the entire Earth starts shaking
The only thing I know
While trying to remain balanced
In the midst of all of this
Is that it will be okay in the end
Because everything always is

    October 31, 2019
    Whately, Massachusetts

What If I Wrote

What if I wrote
The *perfect* line
The *perfect* poem
The *perfect* novel
Would I set my keyboard aside
And simply stop
Because, hey,
No matter what
Nothing I do
Will ever top that?
Of course not
I'll still be here
Doing my thing
Until the end
Because this is what drives me
Not the destination
With the unbeatable view
But the experience of the journey
As I keep on rolling down the road
Not giving it up for anything

    October 31, 2019
    Whately, Massachusetts

October

The Little Hierophant

NOVEMBER

Old New England

The sadness is solidifying
As I am steadily realizing
That the New England I loved
Has become an old New England
Unchanging in the ways I need
Things to be rotationally different
Decaying in the ways I used to like
With the best parts going away
Closing, vanishing right and left
Becoming nothing more than history
Which is not really the best indicator
When you want to settle permanently
And enjoy a place with a good future

     November 10, 2019
     Whately, Massachusetts

November

The Proudly Quippy Smartass

Seeing someone from the past
On social media, fast-forwarded,
Nearly thirty years into the future
Seeing the exact same personality
Shine through as though nothing changed
Still quoting movies from the 80s
Still going on with the wisecracks
Still happily playing the role
Of the proudly quippy smartass
Except what's reaching us is different
As if it were filtered through a layer
Of sadness and crippling loneliness
Projected on a screen weathered,
Crinkled, and clearly saddened
By the emptying of entirely
Too many bottles over
Too many years,
A secret known only
By those who take away
Their recycling every Monday
And those of us who can read it
On their face, in their posts,
And know this isn't going to end well
As the happy-go-lucky mask
Worn for social consumption
Becomes less about the words
And more like a grotesque mirror
Reflecting what's going on inside

    November 10, 2019
    Whately, Massachusetts

I listened to "The Funeral" by Band Of Horses on repeat and wrote.

The Darkness Thoroughly Enjoys

At this time of the year
The darkness thoroughly enjoys
Making us give up
On all of the things we want to do
Simply because it's pitch dark
At five o'clock
And it feels like it's ten
So, honestly why bother
Doing anything at all
When it's clearly time for bed

                November 10, 2019
                Whately, Massachusetts

I love autumn, but I hate this time of the year when it's so dark so early.

November

Finding My Way

Finding my way
Through the densely-packed
Forest of thoughts
It's hard to know
What direction I should go
Because every time my gut
Chooses a direction to follow
The damnable mind butts in
And gives me a million reasons
Why I should stay right here
Or go off somewhere over there
Because of reason and logic
And, it does have valid points
Except my interior compass,
Which has never steered me wrong,
Is frustratingly clear in its
Enunciatingly concise manner
And quietly and politely affirms
That I keep going the way
I feel is right and correct
No matter what my mind might say

November 10, 2019
Whately, Massachusetts

An Effortless Effect

An audience entranced by
The flourishing features
Leading us to believe
In an effortless effect
Quietly concealing the fact
That this astonishing thing took
An amazingly huge amount
Of patience and practice
Miles more than mere mortals
Would want to invest
In something like this

                  November 10, 2019
                  Whately, Massachusetts

November

Ensconced By Handrails

The concept of playing it safe,
Is, in my mind, equally offset
By the idea that we should be
Living as "on the edge" as we
Can
Because the Universe always
Has out back, no matter what
So, keeping our focus on that
We should be jumping off of
Cliffs whenever it's possible
Otherwise
A life lived safely
Where we're ensconced
By handrails
Is not really living
As we're solely focused
On nothing changing
Out of fear that something
Might be disrupted
That we may feel
Or be exposed to
Something, anything
New

                    November 15, 2019
                    Northampton, Massachusetts

Blank Clean

Blank
Clean
A starting space
Unlimited potential
Sometimes it's too overwhelming
For some people
Too many choices
With no direction
Is a torturous hell
But for the creative among us
Blank
Clean
Boundless possibilities
Is nothing short of heaven

                    November 15, 2019
                    Northampton, Massachusetts

I love the possibility that a blank page represents.

November

Faster Than We Can Dream

Time is evaporating
Seemingly quicker than ever
Faster than we can dream
Leaving less opportunity –
Fewer chances for us to achieve

          November 15, 2019
          Northampton, Massachusetts

I will never get used to this.

Living With The Bruises

Standing on the edge of a cliff
Shaped like a peninsula
The only option is to jump
But which side?
They each lead somewhere different
They each have their pros and cons
One is easy and is not that far of a jump
One is a longer jump but still do-able
To an area I am familiar with
The third is so very scary
Filled with uncertainty
But, if I survive,
Has the greatest opportunity
With incredible potential
Now that I think of it, honestly,
What's the point of living life
If you're only existing safely?
If you reach for something big,
Miss, and wind up worse for it
Living with the bruises
Is still better than suffering
Through a lifetime of regret

    November 15, 2019
    Northampton, Massachusetts

November

Now Is The Lull

Now is the lull
Between fall
And the holidays
When we have
Nothing to do
But take stock
Of our lives
If we're unhappy
We'll figure out
How we'll get there
If we're doing great
We'll figure out
How to stay here
So we'll start planning
So on January first
We can start running
Toward better lives

        November 15, 2019
        Northampton, Massachusetts

Risking It

Risking it
To the point
Where it feels
Uncomfortable
Is the place
We need to be
Stepping over
Every boundary
Is just what
We need to do
To quicken the heart
To experience
The feelings denied
This precise moment,
Right here,
Is exactly what we
Need to know
To expand and grow
As the souls we are

        November 16, 2019
        Whately, Massachusetts

November

Your Words Will Be On Walls

Someday your words will be on walls
Either
Quickly applied by spray paint
In a gritty city alleyway
Or
Expertly framed and carefully hung
In a top-tier museum or gallery
If you're lucky
Both will happen simultaneously

        November 16, 2019
        Whately, Massachusetts

This is a mis-mash in my mind of that scene at the end of the movie *Amelie* where the failed writer guy sees his words spray-painted on the side of a building, and how Banksy's art is in auction houses for millions of dollars.

I wrote this while listening to "The Best Thing" by Ivy.

The Reverby Twang

The reverby twang
Surrounding our choices
And the consequences
Echoing somewhat sweetly
Despite the minor key
Edged with the distortion
Of unlikely coincidence
In its rough-hewn way
Giving it that bite
Letting you know
That it all comes
Back to you after
Bouncing around
The room and
When done right
Actually sounds
Pretty damn good

    November 16, 2019
    Whately, Massachusetts

I'm still listening to "The Best Thing" by Ivy on repeat.

I don't know how it's possible that I was completely unaware of this band until now. But, thanks to Spotify, I'm quickly catching up.

November

Disposable

Disposable
Like a straw
Or a plastic fork
That served its purpose
For its one-time use
And is now cast-off
Its usefulness forgotten
Immediately after it's been
Unceremoniously dumped
Tossed aside with the others
Lying on top of the pile
Behind the swinging door
That simply says, "Trash"

    November 21, 2019
    Northampton, Massachusetts

Buy Into

Refusing to pay attention
But will gladly buy into
Anything anyone says
One hundred percent
As long as it fits into their
Razor-thin narrow view
Of the one-town world
Immediately surrounding them

                November 22, 2019
                Northampton, Massachusetts

November

Immutable

This is not the world I once knew
Which has changed beyond belief
In the few short years I've been here
It must be completely unrecognizable
To those who are immutable and incapable
Of changing course and being adaptable
To the too-fast pace we've created

        November 22, 2019
        Northampton, Massachusetts

The Potential

It's the potential
That curiously both
Completely captures,
And sets me free
Just fully knowing
That I can actually do
Pretty much anything
I want because it's all
Going on all around
And totally filling me
With such inspiration
Which ends up becoming
A self-fulfilling prophecy

        November 22, 2019
        Northampton, Massachusetts

November

Traffic Cameras

I love watching
Traffic cameras
Seeing the ebb and flow
Of the cars doing their thing
Studying traffic patterns
And their intimate daily dance
Where the participants think
They're in their private place
In public, but still in their space,
But here I am seeing them
And all the things they are doing
Between the starting and stopping
The comings and goings
Of everyone involved
In the oft-used, very busy,
Stretch of highway
The camera shows me

     November 22, 2019
     Northampton, Massachusetts

The Little Smudge

It's hard to focus on the big picture
When you're obsessing over
The little smudge in the corner
The one no one but you notices

               November 22, 2019
               Northampton, Massachusetts

November

Snowflake

The term "snowflake"
Is most often thrown out
In a demeaning manner
As a slurish put-down
By those who have
The thinnest skin
And are the ones who are
The easiest offended
The quickest triggered
By the faintest words
Daring to intersect their
Unchangingly narrow
Small-town worldview
Thereby bruising
Their delicately sensitive
Sensibilities
And completely ruining
Their entire existence

    November 22, 2019
    Northampton, Massachusetts

New Moon

New moon
More like
No moon
Making astronomers happy
For the clear skies and the
Viewing opportunity
Making astrologers joyful
For the new beginnings
And setting new goals
Making me kind of iffy
For dimming and turning
My backyard creepily dark

                November 25, 2019
                Whately, Massachusetts

November

Past Nouns

Past nouns
Former things
I no longer
Wish to invest
My time
My energy in
In a way
It's like growing up
But the middle age version
Where I've taken stock
Of what surrounds me
Know the direction
Of where I am heading
Jettison the weight
Holding me back
Slowing me down
And I start to haul ass
On my own path
Full of future nouns
Which are mine alone
To discover

                November 25, 2019
                Whately, Massachusetts

The Little Hierophant

Connecting To The Source Of Myself

Connecting to the source of myself
Is like plugging a million strings
Of Christmas lights
Directly into a power plant
Energizing me with such vitality
Powering my motivation
In blasting through my day
Lighting my way
In such color and delight
I never thought was possible
Before I knew I was the end
That plugged into the outlet
Instead of the other side that didn't
Which is why now I'm so bright
And glowing all of the time

           November 25, 2019
           Whately, Massachusetts

November

Speaking In Tongues

Speaking in tongues
Letting my mouth
Move the ways
It's meant to do
Letting the sound
Sound out as to
Express myself, to
Clearly communicate
Candidly and completely
To get the point across
The intensely intimate
Expressions echoing
Secretly, from me
To you, who is open-
Minded and ready
To listen
To receive
The verbiage
I'm trying so hard
To make you see
So you can experience
The world
From my point of view

        November 29, 2019
        Northampton, Massachusetts

I ended up listening to "Speaking In Tongues" by Arcade Fire and David Byrne on repeat (because it's such a great song), and I ended up writing this.

The Most American Of Holidays

Today, Black Friday,
Is the most American of holidays
Where, in order to celebrate,
Most people use a vacation day
Or, take it off without pay
So they can spend money
They don't really have
On things they don't really need
Just because it's that time of year
And the prices are a little lower
To encourage us to liberate our cash
In exchange to be encumbered
With more stuff so our homes
Look like our waistlines –
Growing rapidly
Growing wildly
Filled with the flavor
Of the new, hot, fun things
Going crazy with consumerism
Because that's our culture
And that's just what we do
To commemorate the season

November 29, 2019
Northampton, Massachusetts

November

The Little Hierophant

DECEMBER

The Little Quips

The little quips
That lay bare
Her true feelings
"She was smart
 Because she left"
Which make you
Re-think the mindset
Of the quiet co-worker
You never suspected
Wanted to leave
For something better

                December 6, 2019
                Northampton, Massachusetts

December

Make My Way Up Again

The thing is
I know what to do
I know the steps
I know the processes
I know how it's supposed to go
But, honestly, I jut don't do
Anything with that knowledge
Knowing and having the motivation
To put the ideas into practice
Are so different and so hard
Even when I'm found
Down and crumpled
At the ebbing bottom
Before I can do anything
I have to get up and stand
On my own two feet
And then
Only then
Can I make my way up again

    December 6, 2019
    Northampton, Massachusetts

A Huge Snowman

From a good distance
Way down the street
I see what looks like
A huge snowman
And I'm so impressed,
Excited as I get closer
Wow, look at it…
Then my joy deflates
As I realize it's not
A real snowman after all
Built by happy kids
Or a really fun family –
But a gaudy inflatable
Bought at Walmart

                December 6, 2019
                Northampton, Massachusetts

December

Having Boundless Creativity

Having boundless creativity
Means absolutely nothing
Without the action
Bringing it into reality

>December 6, 2019
>Northampton, Massachusetts

The Decorations Might Not Make It Up

This year the season
Is passing so quickly
That the decorations
Might not make it up
Or be removed from
The box they are in
Sitting in the basement
And I'm okay with it

    December 6, 2019
    Northampton, Massachusetts

December

Goodbye To The Teens

I just realized that we're
Quickly approaching
Not the end of the year
But the end of the decade
Where we will say
Goodbye to the teens
Which I'm happy to leave
And hello to the twenties
To which I wish much luck
May they be happily roaring
Starting on the first of January

    December 6, 2019
    Northampton, Massachusetts

The Fire Under Your Ass

The fire under your ass
Motivating you to move
Had better match
The one in your heart
In intensity and passion
If so
You will conquer the world
If not
You will continue to languish
Right there, where you stand
But with a bum that's burned

                December 6, 2019
                Northampton, Massachusetts

December

Library Mornings

I am the butter
Stealing scenes
Like a loud zipper
Running through
Library mornings
Leaving them better
Than a chef's roux
Without the warnings
Wrapping the sweater

>December 6, 2019
>Northampton, Massachusetts

Sometimes it's fun to write complete and utter nonsense.

The Environment You Choose

The environment you choose
Is the most important thing
As it determines your success –
If you live in a creative desert
Your ideas could wither and die
From lack of inspiration
Or an absence of a community
Which is the fertile soil
Where your concepts grow –
Go to a forest or a jungle
Thick and dense with ideas
And creative thinking
To flourish with experience
And being open to new ideas –
If you are the big fish
Taking up all of a small pond
There's no room to grow
So, become a small fish
In the biggest pond you can find
Giving yourself all the room
To grow and become
The biggest, best version
Of yourself that's possible

    December 9, 2019
    Northampton, Massachusetts

December

I Writhe My Time

Trying to be like a leaf
Open and willing to go
Wherever the winds take me
But also trying something
That's a little more solid
And can help me weather
This, or any, squall
But so far, being both
Has not been working
Because I'm too heavy
For the winds to take me
And I'm far too light
To withstand the storm
So I writhe my time
Being thrashed around
Instead of taking off
Or standing firm
Both of which
Are more preferable
To what I'm suffering

    December 9, 2019
    Northampton, Massachusetts

The Little Hierophant

Between The Sure-Footing Spots

Waiting is the hardest part
The timed-distance spanning
Between the sure-footing spots
Where I was last comfortable
And where I can breathe again

        December 9, 2019
        Northampton, Massachusetts

I wrote this while listening to "Gimmie Shelter" by the Rolling Stones.

December

Ejector Seat

Flying slowly
But I still know
What's coming
Because I can see
What's going on
All around me
I feel the frustration
Of the passed-over
I see the affected
How they're broken
And crushed continually
I see and feel it all
Which is why
I'm gripping the handle
Of my ejector seat
Preparing myself
For the right opportunity
For the right moment
When I feel the adrenaline
Flood right through me
As I pull hard
And in that frozen moment
Everything changes
As the protection around me
Blasts off and is cast away
The rocket under my ass
Fires and jets me upward
Free and clear from
The situation I was in
Flying through the air
Completely on my own
So scary
So thrilling
Feeling life
Beyond the edge of my seat
Feeling the air
Whip around my body

The Little Hierophant

Like an invisible hug
Both high-fiving
And holding me
All at once
From my free-floating vantage
My view has widened immensely
And I benefit from the clarity
I lacked from the cockpit
That sheltered me tightly
Now I have the time
And the space
To see what appeals to me
And choose my landing spot carefully
So I never ever again
Have to settle for anything
Not in alignment
With who I am
Or what I want
Until then
I simply enjoy the moment
Thankful for the view
All around me

        December 12, 2019
        Whately, Massachusetts

Written while listening to "Protection" by Massive Attack.

December

The Smallest Flake

Sometimes the smallest flake
Of a crumb of our deepest dream
Is the hope that can sustain life
Far beyond the buffet of emptiness
We stuff ourselves silly on every day

        December 15, 2019
        Whately, Massachusetts

Caught In The Spray

Caught in the spray
Of the past memories
Spread out in a wide fan
Paused in mid-air
With each drop
Of the wide wave
A separate moment
I can get up close to,
Spread open, look at,
Climb inside,
Experience from every angle
As myself or
As an observer
Millions of drops
Millions of moments
Some bigger
Featuring prominently
Some smaller
Easily forgettable
But every one of them
There, in perfect clarity
Like a museum
Filled with the frames
Featuring and
Showing the entirety
Of my existence

December 16, 2019
Northampton, Massachusetts

Flip The Page Over Into January

Looking at the calendar
Which may as well say
"Dead End" on it
Because we're down to
Just two weeks remaining
Of the year
Of the decade
And each of those weeks
Has a holiday sitting in it
Which we all know
Negates any actual work
So, the hope of cramming
Everything I was intending
To get done in the remainder
Is foolish and imprudent
I may as well shrug and
Give up on the rest of the year
And focus my attention
At hitting the ground running
When we flip the page over
Into January

December 16, 2019
Northampton, Massachusetts

A Brittle Twig

Opportunity here is like a brittle twig
Tentatively ready to snap at any moment
Where there is nothing new, no adventure
Just history, just past places and people
Which, I guess is fine for a while
But, at some point, I need to experience
Something new, like points of view
And new scenes to point a camera at
Instead of the same-old I've seen
Too many times to count over the years
Each time, more shine is gone
Replaced with the rusting and fading
Painted by time in this performance piece
Whose central tenant is degrading
Which is why, for me, I step firmly –
Snapping the twig
Stepping in a new direction
One with hope and opportunity
Breathing and teeming with life
And the magical awesomeness of creation

                December 22, 2019
                Whately, Massachusetts

I am trusting my gut and following my heart.

December

I Like How The Neighbor Keeps His Outdoor Christmas Trees Lit At Night

I don't know his name
When I see him, I waive, but
I like how the neighbor keeps his
Outdoor Christmas trees lit at night
The evergreens wrapped in lights
Spreading their joy at all times
8pm, 4am, or anytime it's dark
Shining just for me
When I get up early
Taking the dog to pee
So I take a moment to express
How thankful I am for them
Before looking up at the stars
The other lights on all night
And appreciate their consistency
Which will last long past
The holiday season
Always up
Always on
Always there
Always

                December 22, 2019
                Whately, Massachusetts

A Regular Day

The lead-up to the day
Felt muted this year
Maybe it's that I don't
Have cable, so I'm not exposed
To the barrage of commercials
Reminding us that Christmas
Is coming and when it falls
Or, that I don't listen to the radio
So I'm not inundated with
Wall-to-wall Christmas music
Maybe it's that I don't have kids
To constantly pester me to buy presents
Or maybe it's none of the above
Whatever the reason
Today felt like a regular day
Except I had it off from work
And the roads were nicely quiet

    December 25, 2019
    Whately, Massachusetts

Band Names From The 1980s

Band names from the 1980s
Were a weird thing of beauty
Stranger than anything
Anyone could have made up
Showing their creativity
And pure fearlessness
Of the musicians back then
Who were happy being known
By their oddball names
Back when life was fun
And comparatively carefree

                December 27, 2019
                Northampton, Massachusetts

My Penmanship

My penmanship
Has declined greatly,
Due to the keyboard
I have no consistency
With my handwriting
I'm taking shortcuts
With the loops on my 2s
Which used to be robust
Now they're flattened
And barely there
The same with the
Vertical lines on my 5s
Being more curved
And so very short
They look more like Ss
For the sake of speed
Which will never match
What my fingers can do
Thanks to technology
And the modern keyboard

    December 27, 2019
    Northampton, Massachusetts

Look Better On Paper

The desire to help
And do, be, better
Is fueled by the need
To make their metrics
Look better on paper
With marketable PR
That can be used to sell
The company, the brand,
And nothing else

        December 27, 2019
        Northampton, Massachusetts

I Was Born Way Back

Someday someone
Might look at my birth year
And make a horrified face
Thinking about how
I was born way back
In the painfully archaic
Nineteen hundreds
Not just least century
But last millennium
Back before YouTube,
Smartphones, and
Giant skinny televisions
When clouds were
In the sky and not a place
We stored our valuables
Much in the same way
I think about my great-grandfather
And how he was born
In the eighteen hundreds
Before life was "normal," and…
Maddeningly complicated

    December 28, 2019
    Whately, Massachusetts

December

Puddle Now

Puddle now
Wet and splashy
Frozen later
Slippery and icy
Water has a hard time
Making up its mind
Changing forms
Solid, liquid, gas
Depending completely
On the whims of the weather
Instead of following
It's own heart
And just sticking
With what feels right

            December 28, 2019
            Whately, Massachusetts

All Of This Speaks Of Spring

It's the end of December
But it feels like the end of March
With the snow receding
Showing the fields, the lawns
The land that's been covered
For only a few weeks now
But honestly, it still seems like
We've endured a full winter already
But the heat of the sunshine
Squinting my smiling face,
The running water dripping
From the roof, puddling
Out from under snow banks
That are clearly shrinking
The squishening ground –
All of this speaks of spring
Which is still a full season away
But has decided to give us a preview
Today, and for the foreseeable future
And normally I would be concerned,
Because this is not normal in any way,
But honestly, right now, I don't care
It just feels so nice
To not be freezing,
Slipping, or shoveling

December 28, 2019
Whately, Massachusetts

December

This Was Meant To Be Seen

The scene hanging
Outside there
Out the window
Looking like something
Found in a beginner art class
Sunsetting tonight on canvas
Where the Decembered silhouetted tree
Leafless and comprised of nothing
But naked individual branches
Thinning out, radiating into twigs
In the too-perfect oblonged curve
Prominently in the foreground
With the jutting craggily horizon
Of the far distant trees
Providing the dark shelf
For everything above to sit on
Contrasting too ideally
With the wide, flat clouds
Expertly reflecting
The last filtered vestiges
Of the day's long-gone light
Backlighting the scene
With such a vibrancy and intensity
Clearly outshining, and re-defining
The name formally used by
The shame-filled fruit
Whose deeply-rooted embarrassment
At being so dull and lifeless
Compared to the energetic scene
Of orange exploding,
Burning the midriff
Of the sky itself
Upon which Nature herself
Confidently declared
This Was Meant To Be Seen
Until the eyes look upward
To the cooling pale blue

The Little Hierophant

Darkening up to inky navy
To the heightening depth
Where the stars dwell
Yawning off their daytime slumber
While you're here, blown away
By all this, encompassed in one glance
Designed to seriously wow
And be appreciated in the moment
Too simple to be a good painting
Too beautiful to cheapen the experience
With anything other than eyes
Since it was changing too quickly
With each passing second
And, before you could tell anyone,
The light, the scene, the fire
Was drained, muted, and gone

    December 28, 2019
    Whately, Massachusetts

I was just looking at the sunset photo I posted on my Instagram account (on December 24, 2019) and started to write about it. Some poems I can just write effortlessly, but this one took probably three hours over the course of the afternoon with a long break in-between writing to clear my mind.

At The End

I'm here
At the end
Of the month
Of the year
Of the decade
All of which
I am firmly
Done and through with,
This too-long night,
And more than ready
To move past from
Into the twenties
Into the future
Bright like the dawn
Spectacular and promising
But at the moment
When it all resets
I will be asleep
So I can be fully
Rested and ready
To rise early
And get going
On the new path
As fast as I can go
While everyone else
Is deeply sleeping

        December 31, 2019
        Whately, Massachusetts

Goodbye 2019!

The Little Hierophant

IF YOU ENJOYED THIS COLLECTION

Please consider rating it at Amazon.com. As an independent author, having people review my works is critical in helping to increase my exposure and letting new people discover books like this. Thank you!

WRITTEN BY ERIC NIXON

The Little Hierophant – 2019 poetry collection
Equidistant – 2018 poetry collection
The Cupcake – 2017 poetry collection
2492: Attack Of The Ancient Cyborg – science fiction novel
The Ocean Above – 2016 poetry collection
Cascadia's Fault – 2015 poetry collection
The Taborist – 2014 poetry collection
The Entire Universe – 2013 poetry collection
Trying Not To Blink – 2012 poetry collection
Lost In Thought – poetry collection
Emily Dickinson – Superhero: Vol. 1 – historical fiction novel
Incident On The Hennepin – a short story set in *2492*
Plenty Of Time – a short story
Retribution On A Jetpack – a short story set in *2492*
Anything But Dreams – poetry collection

Available at Amazon.com/author/ericnixon

ABOUT THE AUTHOR

Eric Nixon is a poet and author who has written ten collections of poetry, several short stories, and a two novels – *2492: Attack Of The Ancient Cyborg* and *Emily Dickinson, Superhero: Vol. 1*. Eric lives in western Massachusetts.

www.ingramcontent.com/pod-product-compliance
Lightning Source LLC
LaVergne TN
LVHW041247080426
835510LV00009B/628